Rugby's Berlin Wall
League and Union from 1895 to today

Amateur rugby league: Ipswich Rhinos versus South Asia Bulls
– Middlesex Nines 2004. (Photo: Peter Lush)

By Graham Williams, Peter Lush and David Hinchliffe

LONDON LEAGUE PUBLICATIONS Ltd

Rugby's Berlin Wall
League and Union from 1895 to today

© Copyright Graham Williams, Peter Lush and David Hinchliffe
Foreword © Huw Richards, introduction © David Hinchliffe

Cover design © Stephen McCarthy. Photographs © the photographer or contributor of the photograph.

Front cover photos: Top: Bradford Bulls versus Leeds Rhinos 2004 Super League action (Photo: Peter Lush). Bottom: Leeds Tykes Rugby Union Powergen Cup winners 2005 (Photo: David Williams)
Back cover: Rugby Raiders versus Wolverhampton Wizards – The Raiders first match played at Rugby School, refereed by Russell Smith (Photo: Peter Lush)

A CIP catalogue record for this book is available from the British Library.

First published in Great Britain in September 2005 by:
London League Publications Ltd, P.O. Box 10441, London E14 8WR

ISBN: 1-903659-23-X

Cover design by: Stephen McCarthy Graphic Design
                               46, Clarence Road, London N15 5BB

Layout: Peter Lush

Printed and bound by: Antony Rowe Ltd
                               Chippenham, Wiltshire, Great Britain

Foreword

That the cultural barriers between rugby's two codes remain so strong a decade after the institutional ones were swept away in union's lurch into open professionalism merely serves to underline what the more perceptive historians have long argued - that it was only ever incidentally about money.

Class, perception and the on-field divergence of the two codes over more than a century of separation - for a longer than the period for which they were a single game - have proved to be far more significant in maintaining the gulf between them.

That gap, as deep as the division between the 'two cultures' of science and the liberal arts identified by novelist C. P. Snow in the 1950s, is reflected in continuing mutual incomprehension which can verge upon the comical. During the brief flurry of high-profile transfers three or four years ago it was hard to know which was the more unwittingly hilarious - the Home Counties-based scribes who insisted that the loss of a couple of high-profile players spelt the doom of a code, although the Welsh union had survived the transfer of more than 300 between the wars, or the voices from Warrington, Wakefield and Workington proclaiming mortal outrage that anyone should stoop so low as to offer somebody money to change codes.

Incomprehension extends to more factual matters. For the uninformed union followers' conviction that league is exclusively professional, read his league doppelganger's belief that top-class union is watched by three men and a dog. The better-informed of course are well aware that the bulk of league in the UK is played under the auspices of the British Amateur Rugby League Association, whose rigour over professionalism matches anything formerly practised by the rulers of the other game, while gates in Super League and rugby union's Premiership have marched more-or-less in step over the past few seasons.

It is similarly unacknowledged that 1895, whose importance needs no explaining for league fans, is just as important a date in union's development. It gave union an underpinning ideology, a safety-valve (although as Graham Williams notes, the more unreconstructed unionists, ultra-reactionary British Lions manager James Baxter in 1930 following Arthur Budd's usage of the 1890s, preferred to call it a sewer) and an 'other' against which to define itself.

All three factors ensured that union remained officially amateur for far longer than would be the case. The hypocrisies this entailed - the suppression of French league under Vichy, the same Rowe Harding who had proudly proclaimed his 1920s Cambridge team 'professional gladiators' solely devoted to victory over Oxford, saying in 1951 that while league in Wales was 'only an infant, it wants strangling' and of course the regulation that allowed Welsh kicker Paul Thorburn to trial with an unquestionably professional American Football Club while banning Ady Spencer for playing as an amateur - are well-known to historically aware league followers. It is worth noting here the presence of two future secretaries of the Rugby Football Union - Robin Prescott and Bob Weighell - among the forwards in the Rugby Union Combined Services team beaten at Odsal in 1944.

Both games can be glad that these hypocrisies have gone (even if French Rugby League awaits the return of a more sympathetic government before the report commissioned into its wartime suppression is made public). Both, particularly union, are healthier for it. At the same time, it was possible to understand why league fans feared for the future of their game and saw union as a predatory, potentially destructive force as its stars were targeted.

There is, though, little reason to worry. The history of the different, competing, football codes is that once one is firmly established in a district or region it takes a great deal of displacing. League knows this to its own cost, in the endless travails it has suffered in its attempts to take the professional game far beyond the boundaries of 1895. Union struggles to break out of college-sustained enclaves in North America while soccer, at professional level at least, also remains a marginal presence in the USA and Canada. Association football made few inroads in Yorkshire before the schism of 1895 left rugby weakened.

The assumption that once professionalism ceased to be an issue rugby's two codes must invariably converge and merge echoes the misplaced conviction once expressed by a friend of mine, an enthusiastic admirer of all things American, that he 'couldn't really see what Canadian nationhood was about and surely it would soon become part of the USA'. He had of course homed in on the one thing that the citizens of that fractured, often dysfunctional state stretching from Vancouver to Halifax by way of Quebec could agree on - that whatever else they might want - they certainly do not wish to be Americans.

Similarly with rugby league fans. They too are a memorably fissiparous and disputatious lot - as Dave Hadfield points out in that wonderfully perceptive mix of travelogue, memoir and meditation *Up and Over*, league has much in common with the political left. Where most sports have enthusiasts, league has activists who offer both the advantages of commitment and the downside of a marked propensity to fall out over matters both personal and doctrinal. That this tendency has more to do with the game than any regional characteristics was illustrated by the remarkable talent for falling out among themselves displayed by the committed activists who sustained Fulham / London Crusaders through the decade between Fulham FC's withdrawal and the Brisbane takeover.

But whatever else they argue about; league fans are agreed on one thing. They do not want rugby union. Whenever league fans have been polled on the future of the game, a merger with union has shown up in lost deposit territory. Union fans are little different - perverse as it may seem to league followers, they like rucks, lines-out and genuine scrums and would regard their game as diminished by the loss of any of them.

The codes will doubtless continue to skirmish along their borders. The occasional, sometimes high-profile, player will switch - supporters of both games will regard Saracens FC's early fixtures in late 2005 with particular interest as Andrew Farrell attempts to make the leap. There may be the odd inter-code challenge match - hamstrung by the difficulty that these events only have popular appeal if played by the highest-profile teams and players, so that they invariably involve matching talented novices with opponents too good even for most highly-competent professional specialists in that particular code. The main lesson of the Bath versus Wigan games in 1996 was the extent to which the two codes had diverged - Graham Williams, while undoubtedly writing from a league viewpoint shows an even-handedness unusual in commentators from either side on these two games in pointing not only to Wigan's undoubted superiority with the ball in hand but also to the fact, rarely acknowledged by league writers, that Bath unquestionably held back in scrummages in the union clash.

We may even see occasional attempts to devise combined rules, in the same spirit that has seen Australian Football and Gaelic Football compensate for their dearth of international opponents by inventing a hybrid game for an annual series of challenge matches. Such attempts, though, are doomed to founder on the tackle law - the simple, straightforward division between the two codes from which all else follows. If the ball remains in play after a tackle, you are playing union. If it does not, the game is league.

Both games, having signed so much of themselves over to Rupert Murdoch, have reason to be wary of television magnates who may be more concerned about the possibility of a quick buck than the sensibilities of those who prize what make their games distinctive. Murdoch's greatest need, though, is for instant action to fill the space between the adverts on his ever-growing satellite television channels. To try to turn two games into one, reducing the hours of product available, would make no sense.

League will always keep a wary eye on union - history alone ensures that. But so long as there are people who want to play rugby league, and others who want to watch it, there can be no doubt that it will survive.

Huw Richards
July 2005

Huw Richards is the rugby correspondent of the *Financial Times*, and covers both codes with equal enthusiasm and knowledge. His most recent book is *Dragons and All Blacks*, published by Mainstream.

Introduction

For followers of either code of rugby, the last decade has probably been the most momentous period in the history of their sport since the original split between the two in the 19th century.

The year 1995 had been scheduled by the Rugby Football League for the celebration of their game's centenary. But it turned into a year of the most remarkable contemporary developments which would set the course for the direction of both rugby league and rugby union for many years to come.

Firstly, rugby league took the highly controversial step of agreeing a lucrative broadcasting deal with Rupert Murdoch's BSkyB to form a 12 team Super League and move the sport in England from winter to summer.

Secondly, - and almost 100 years to the day since the original division of the codes - rugby union took the decision to become openly professional.

For anyone even remotely interested in either game what followed these remarkable upheavals has, in itself, been worthy of being labelled a spectator sport. The original Super League vision of what Peter Lush in Chapter Four terms "a competition based in big cities, with an international pan-European dimension" came into immediate conflict with the views of many rugby league traditionalists who saw the sport's strengths as its roots in the local communities of Northern England. Within rugby union there was an inevitable tension between the traditional emphasis on the enjoyment of participation and the new era of intense professional competition which emphasised the need to improve the on-field product for the increasingly important paying spectator.

But of particular fascination was to be the way what had been sport's bitterest rivals for a century would relate to each other when the formal barrier of the amateur - professional divide had finally been removed.

This book is a collection of essays which aim to examine the nature of that relationship in the decade which has followed the ground-breaking decisions of 1995. It seeks to place the developments of that year and since in their historical context. The authors believe that to fully understand the significance of what happened then, it is vital to also have an appreciation of what was happening within and between the codes over the previous century and more. Understanding the past might also make it easier to anticipate what will happen within that relationship in the future.

There are few other issues in sport that have generated more argument and heated debate than the relative merits of rugby league and rugby union.

Supporters of both games have been engaged in an intense and bitter tribal warfare since the great divide of the late 1800s. Those of us who were subject to what Graham Williams in Chapter Two calls "the rugby equivalent of eternal damnation" - being banned for life from one sport for having played another - won't easily forget. And on the other side of the coin, those who saw their best players enticed from club and country by the financial rewards of another game won't easily forgive.

But now that the central bone of contention - professionalism - is no longer the key dividing factor where does it leave the individual identities of these traditionally separate tribes? What, if anything, can we learn from past events - and especially the developments of the last 10 years - which might enable us to better anticipate the future for both codes of rugby? Indeed, will there still be two codes or, just as the events of the 1890s paved the way for the split, might those of 100 years later have set the scene for an eventual reunification?

David Hinchliffe
July 2005

Thank you

London League Publications Ltd and the authors would like to thank: Steve McCarthy for his work on the cover; the staff of Antony Rowe Ltd for printing the book; David Williams of RLPhotos.com and Robert Gate for providing photos and Jed Smith of the Museum of Rugby, Twickenham, for permission to reproduce "Rules as to Professionalism". Naturally, we take responsibility for any mistakes in the book.

About the authors

Graham Williams has been following rugby league in general and Leeds in particular for over 30 years. To the consternation of some of his friends he has also followed the City's rugby union teams. For the past 20 years or so he has been delving into aspects of rugby league's history, especially those surrounding its attempts at expansion and its struggles with both association football and rugby union. During that time he has contributed articles to a number of club programmes, *Open Rugby*, *Code 13*, *Our Game* and has published a couple of books examining the rugby game's evolution.

Peter Lush was introduced to rugby league at Craven Cottage in 1980 by Dave Farrar. Since then he has become a great supporter of the game, and fascinated by its history. In 1995, with Dave Farrar, he launched London League Publications Ltd, and published their first book, *Touch and Go*. The company has now published 23 books about the game. In 2000, they launched *Our Game*, a rugby league magazine covering both current issues and the sport's history. He also follows association football, supporting West Ham United and Hendon, and cricket, supporting Middlesex CCC. He works as a trade union outreach worker and freelance consultant in the voluntary and social housing sectors.

David Hinchliffe played amateur rugby league for many years and is a life-long follower of Wakefield Trinity RLFC. He was Wakefield's Labour MP from 1987 to 2005 and was chairman of the Commons Health Select Committee during the last two Parliaments. He was one of the founders of the All-Party Parliamentary Rugby League Group and acted as its Secretary for sixteen years. He was the author of *Rugby's Class War* and editor of *A Westminster XIII*. Away from politics and sport he has a passion for genealogy and local history as well as travelling the northern waterways on his family's narrow boat.

Contents

This book was very much a joint effort, with much debate and exchange of ideas. Graham Williams wrote chapters 2, 5, 6 and 8; Peter Lush wrote chapters 1, 3 and 4, and David Hinchliffe wrote chapter 7. Some of the research for Chapter 1 was done by Gavin Willacy for an article in *Our Game*.

RULES AS TO
PROFESSIONALISM

The Rugby Union Committee deem it advisable, as the game spreads in all parts of the country, to draw the attention of all players to these rules.

THE PRINCIPAL RULES AS AFFECT THE INDIVIDUAL ARE AS FOLLOWS:—

1. Professionalism is illegal.
2. Acts of Professionalism are:—

   Asking, receiving, or relying on a promise, direct or implied, to receive any money consideration whatever, actual or prospective, any employment or advancement, any establishment in business, or any compensation whatever for:—

   (a) Playing football or rendering any service to a football organisation (provided however, that the Secretary and Treasurer of a Club who has definitely ceased playing football may be excepted under special conditions).

   (b) Training, or loss of time connected therewith.

   (c) Time lost in playing football or in travelling in connection with football.

   (d) Expenses in excess of the amount actually disbursed on account of reasonable hotel or travelling expenses.

   Playing for a Club while receiving, or after having received from such Club, any consideration whatever for acting as an official, or for doing or having done any work about the Club's ground or in connection with the Club's affairs, unless such work was done before the receiver became a football player.

   Remaining on tour at his Club's expense longer than is reasonable.

   Giving or receiving any money testimonial. Or, giving or receiving any other testimonial, except under the authority of this Union.

   Playing on any ground where gate money is taken:—

   (a) During the close season (that is between 21st April and 1st September, except when the Tuesday in Easter Week falls later than 21st April, when the close season shall commence from the Wednesday in the Easter Week), except where special permission for the game has been granted by this Committee.

   (b) In any match or contest where it is previously agreed that less than 15 players on each side shall take part (except where, in exceptional cases, this Committee may have granted special permission for less than 15 players aside to take part).

   Knowingly playing with or against any expelled or suspended player or Club, or with or against any professional player or Club.

   Refusing to give evidence or otherwise assist in carrying out these rules when requested by this Union to do so.

   Being registered as, or declared a professional, or suspended by any National Rugby Union or by the Football Association.

   Playing within 8 days of any accident for which he has claimed or received insurance compensation, if insured under these rules.

   Playing in any benefit match connected with football (except where this Committee has given permission for a *bona fide* charity match).

   Knowingly playing or acting as referee or touch judge on the ground of an expelled or suspended club.

   Receiving money or other valuable consideration from any person or persons as an inducement towards playing football.

   Signing any form of the Northern Union (Rugby League).

   Advocating or taking steps to promote Northern Union (Rugby League) or other professional football.

   The penalty for breach of these Rules is suspension or expulsion. (Expulsion carries with it the formal declaration of professionalism).

   This Union shall have power to deal with all acts which it may consider as acts of professionalism and which are not specifically provided for.

   October, 1924.   *BY ORDER OF THE COMMITTEE.*

IGNORANCE OF THE RULES IS NO DEFENCE.

Rugby Union's rules on 'professionalism' in 1924
(Courtesy Museum of Rugby, Twickenham.)

Part One: Amateurs and professionals

Richard Lockwood (Dewsbury & England rugby union.)
(Photo: Courtesy London League Publications Ltd)

Lewis Jones – the golden boy of Welsh rugby union in the early 1950s who
then had a wonderful rugby league career for Leeds and Great Britain.
(Photo: Courtesy Robert Gate)

1. Before the split:
Rugby union in Yorkshire and Lancashire before 1895

The events and disputes leading up to the formation of the Northern Union in 1895 have been well analysed elsewhere. However, to understand the relationship between the two codes as it developed after 1895, it is important to look at the development of rugby union in Yorkshire and Lancashire up to 1895, and what the departure of the clubs in 1895 to the Northern Union meant for rugby union. Both areas were important centres for the sport. The development of clubs through competitions improved playing standards, and gradually more northern players appeared in the England team.

The 22 clubs that formed the Northern Union in 1895 were evenly split between Lancashire and Yorkshire, including some that were in Cheshire under the 'Lancashire' banner. Most of the clubs had competed in the senior county leagues that had been formed in Yorkshire and Lancashire, and in the Yorkshire Cup, which was clearly a factor in their decision to join the Northern Union, as well as the issue of 'broken time'. It was these senior county leagues which formed the basis of the Northern Union competition in 1895.

One possible measure of the strength of rugby football in different areas of the country prior to 1895 is the county championship. In 1888-89, the RU gave the County Championship official recognition.

However, before then, the Reverend Frank Marshall, a noted rugby union historian, and great advocate of 'amateurism', said that only Middlesex, Lancashire and Yorkshire could "put forward a legitimate claim for such distinction" and Middlesex did not play many matches. From 1881 to 1884, Yorkshire only lost once, and Marshall said "may fairly be considered champion."

In 1884-85, Lancashire could claim the title, and although other counties challenged the two northern giants more strongly in the second half of the decade, they still played a leading role.

In 1888-89, Yorkshire won all their six matches, and claimed 11 places in the North versus South match. Yorkshire were unbeaten in 1889-90, but drew twice, with Middlesex and Cheshire.

In 1890-91, the title stayed in the north, but crossed the Pennines, going to Lancashire, who won all their nine matches. Yorkshire took back their title the next year, and continued to dominate the competition for the next two years, winning 15 out of 17 matches against other counties, with two draws.

Yorkshire retained their title in 1894-95, and as champion county, they defeated the Rest of England at Headingley in April 1895.

The Yorkshire Union

Bradford, Huddersfield and Hull along with Leeds (not the current rugby league club) set up the Yorkshire Union in 1874; three years after the Rugby Union (RU) had been formed in 1871. York soon got involved, and in 1876, the Yorkshire Union agreed to launch the Yorkshire Challenge Cup. The first competition was held in the 1877-78 season, with Halifax beating York in the final. From then until 1895, Halifax won the cup four more times, Wakefield Trinity also won it on four occasions, and six other clubs who would join the NU in 1895 also won it on one occasion. Only three times were clubs who stayed with the RU in 1895 successful.

Hull FC was formed in 1865, six years before the RU itself. The club was set up by former public schoolboys. However, according to the Reverend Frank Marshall, in his seminal book *Football – The Rugby Union Game*, "the game played was neither the regular Rugby nor the Association game, but one something resembling Rugby, though running with the ball was only permitted after a catch." Two Hull players, William Hutchinson, known as 'The Baron' and Gilbert Harrison captained Yorkshire, and both also played for England. Harrison won seven England caps between 1877 and 1885, and Hutchinson played for England twice. Four Hull players were in the first Yorkshire team that played Lancashire in 1870.

However, Hull never won the Yorkshire Cup while playing rugby union. In 1883 they reached the final, losing to Bradford at Leeds St Johns, in front of a 15,000 crowd.

A rugby club was formed in Leeds in 1864. However, the forerunner of today's rugby league club was the Leeds St John's club, who were formed in 1870. In 1890, they moved to Headingley, and became the football section of the Leeds Cricket, Football & Athletic Company. Headingley became a regular venue for Yorkshire Cup finals. In 1891, 17,720 fans attended the final, with 17,288 present in 1893. Although attendances for the 1894 and 1895 finals fell slightly, to 16,093 and 14,038, these crowds show the strength of support for the Yorkshire Cup.

Bradford was formed in 1868, as an offshoot of Bradford Cricket Club. However, meetings were being held by the footballers from 1863, and according to Marshall "framed a code of rules for themselves, the Rugby Union not having then come into existence." Again, the game was a mixture of association football and rugby. They played in the Park Avenue area, and the roots of Bradford Northern are found in this club. There was a split in 1907, when the Bradford club switched to association football. Members who wished to continue playing rugby formed a new club, which soon adopted the Bradford Northern name to distinguish itself from the association football club.

Bradford's leading member in this period was Harry Garnett. He captained the club from 1874 to 1881, captained Yorkshire from 1877 to

1880, and was a member of the Yorkshire Union committee for 18 years, including seven as president. Bradford's best period was 1883 to 1885, when they were "the premier club in England". These years included their sole Yorkshire Cup win, in 1884. John Toothill played 10 times for England between 1890 and 1984, when Yorkshire based players played a major role in the England team, and Tommy Dobson was also capped by England in 1895.

Huddersfield

Huddersfield was formed in 1864. In the 1870s, the Huth brothers were the driving force behind the team. Harry was capped by England, and with his brothers Fred and Frank played for Yorkshire. The team's fortunes declined after their retirement, but revived for their sole Yorkshire Cup win in 1890, when they defeated the powerful Wakefield Trinity by a goal to nil. Other Huddersfield players to win England honours before 1895 included Ernest Woodward and J. Dyson.

The York club dated from 1872-73. York reached the first Yorkshire Cup Final, in 1877, but were easily beaten by Halifax, who mustered a goal, a try and nine touchdowns to nil. Marshall's comments on York could apply in modern times: "York has suffered much through lack of a good ground, and from the loss of good players, whose term of service to the club has been brief, either owing to injury or migration."

Halifax first played a match in December 1873, when they only had 10 members. They were the most successful team in the Yorkshire Cup up to 1895, and Marshall says: "The Halifax team has always taken a prominent part in the tussle for the cup. One of their best players was George Thomas Thompson. He was "a strong, slashing player, especially good at the line-out and in the open, being a very strong runner, and generally going straight, and having but few tricks; he was a most difficult man to stop, handling an opponent off well." Despite this description of his play, he was said to be of a "genial disposition" and was the "idol of Yorkshire" until he moved south in 1885.

Another of Yorkshire's great clubs who joined the Northern Union was Wakefield Trinity. Formed in 1873, they won the Yorkshire Cup four times before the split, and appeared in nine finals. Apparently their best team in these early years was "that beaten in the cup ties of 1884 by Heckmondwike in a mud hole on the Heckmondwike ground by a goal to two tries." Marshall says that they "are noted for playing a cup tie game. They have brought to perfection the science of obtaining little advantages and keeping them... The style is not pretty but it is very clever and nonplusses the opposing side."

One of their leading players was Teddy Bartram, who "will be best remembered for his inventive genius in discovering loopholes in the laws, especially as regards the trick of picking up and dropping at goal after a try obtained in an unfavourable position." Their first international was Barron Kilner, who played for England against Ireland in 1880. Herbert Fallas won a cap in 1884, and Fred Laurie was capped in 1889 and 1890. In 1882-83, Rowland Hill, the RU's secretary, said that "the Trinity club was second to no other club in England."

Dewsbury were founded in October 1875. One of their most distinguished players was Richard (Dicky) Lockwood, who was "unquestionably the finest all-round wing threequarter of the present day." Dewsbury were also represented in the Yorkshire Rugby Union, with Mark Newsome being the first president of the Union from 1888 to 1890, and being a member of the RU's international board. His brother Alfred also played for Dewsbury, and his left-foot drop goal won the Yorkshire Cup for his team in 1881. He was "a strong dashing runner, never going out of his way when making for the goal line, but handing off right and left and changing the ball accordingly. He never had his equal, at least in Yorkshire, at this style of play; he certainly was a terror."

Other clubs who joined the Northern Union included Bramley, who were founded in 1879, and joined the NU in 1896; Hull KR, founded in 1883 and who moved to the NU in 1897, and Batley, who were founded in 1880 and joined the NU in 1895. Bramley had three England rugby union internationals, Charlie Mathers, who went on the first international tour to Australasia, H. Bradshaw, who won seven caps from 1892 to 1894, and W. 'Bobby' Whitley.

Lancashire

Of the 10 clubs that entered the Lancashire Club Championship in 1894-95, six of the seven who finished the season in the competition joined the Northern Union, and Swinton followed them in 1896. The other three teams - Leigh, Salford and Wigan – were suspended for professionalism. Leigh and Wigan joined the Northern Union in 1895, Salford following in 1896.

The Northern Union initially did not make the same impact on the other side of the Pennines in Lancashire. Rugby in the county was dominated initially by the Manchester club, and the Lancashire Football Union was set up in 1881 initially without their co-operation. It was soon renamed the Lancashire County Football Club when Manchester agreed to get involved. However, Swinton, Oldham and Rochdale Hornets were all present at the initial meeting. In 1889, Warrington and Wigan were involved in meetings to expand the structure of the Lancashire County. Two years later, 12 of the clubs listed as members of County Club joined the NU in its early years. It is interesting to note that neither the Manchester or Liverpool clubs switched to the NU, and rugby league has never established a strong presence in either of these cities.

Arthur Crook, who wrote the chapter in Marshall's book on Lancashire, says that "Rochdale Hornets must certainly be included amongst the early pioneers of the game in Lancashire, and are to be congratulated today in occupying a front place amongst the chief clubs in the county. He says that in the early 1870s, outside Manchester and Liverpool, the only strong rugby clubs were in Preston and Rochdale. Rochdale Hornets were founded in 1871, and the town became a hotbed for the game, with 57 clubs in the town and district in 1881.

He outlines that Swinton were originally an association football club, switched to rugby in 1870, and "certainly no organisation in England has enjoyed a more singularly uninterrupted run of success." He says the club is the "foremost" in Lancashire, and it plays the "strongest opponents in the country." In 1877-78, Swinton played the famous Manchester club for the first time, and beat them in front of a 4,500 crowd at Manchester's Whalley Range ground. This result came in a period when Swinton were unbeaten for three seasons.

Two of Swinton's most prominent players were Edward (Ted) Beswick, who played for Lancashire many times after his debut in 1879, and represented England; and James Valentine, who made his Lancashire debut in 1884, and played for England in 1890. Crook's chapter concentrates more on players than clubs. Another he mentions is Thomas Kent, who won Lancashire and England honours while a Salford player. Other England internationals from Swinton include Charlie Horley, who was capped in 1884-85, James Marsh and Sam Roberts. The club was also regularly represented in the Lancashire county team.

Proposals for a Lancashire Cup were considered by the County in the 1880s, but were defeated. There was a county league championship from 1893, but this collapsed after the Northern Union was established. Salford were the winners in 1892-93, and Oldham in 1893-94.

Salford had been founded in 1873. In 1881, they merged with another local club, The Crescent FC, which considerably strengthened the club. By 1886, they were becoming one of the stronger clubs in Lancashire, and had a 21 match unbeaten run. The next year, they improved this by one, with a 22 match run. One of their stars was Harry Eagles, who was selected for England in 1888, but did not play as the RFU were in dispute with the other unions. He was selected for the 1888 Great Britain tour to Australia and New Zealand, and appeared in all 52 matches. Three other Salford players: Jack Anderton, Tom Kent and Sam Williams were also selected for the tour. Fourteen out of 22 players on that tour were from clubs who later joined the Northern Union.

Kent was also selected for England, winning six England caps from 1891 to 1892. Numerous Salford players also played for Lancashire. In 1890-91, the Salford team had two internationals and six county players. The club itself had 2,100 members.

Oldham, who won the county league championship in 1893-94, were another strong Lancashire club who were to join the Northern Union. The club was founded in 1876, and in 1888 signed two Welsh internationals, Dai Gwyn and Bill McCutcheon. They both won more Welsh caps while with Oldham in the 1890s. For England, Ab Ashworth was capped in 1892 against Ireland. Oldham were also well represented in the Lancashire team, with 17 players achieving representative honours.

Other Lancashire clubs who joined the Northern Union included St Helens, who were founded in 1873, and Warrington, who were founded in 1879. Broughton Rangers were founded as Broughton in 1877, and a merger of two other local clubs in 1878 meant a change of name to Broughton Rangers in 1878. Bob Seddon, Arthur Teggin and Arthur Royle all won England rugby union honours with the club, and their team of 1886 had five Lancashire players. In 1892, they caused a sensation by signing Welsh internationals David and Evan James from Swansea. Allegations of professionalism were soon made, and after a handful of games for the Rangers, in January 1893 they were suspended for three years. They returned to Wales, played as amateurs again, including for Wales in 1899, before returning to Broughton, this time in the Northern Union.

The winners of the Lancashire club championship in 1894-95 were Tyldesley. They were founded in 1879, and in 1887-88 signed a famous half-back, Buff Berry. In 1890-91, he won three England caps, and was an ever-present in the Lancashire team that won the County Championship for the first time. Two other players also won Lancashire honours. The club joined the Northern Union in 1895, but only survived until 1901 due to low crowds and lack of funds.

It would be wrong to say that rugby union was wiped out in Yorkshire and Lancashire by the formation of the Northern Union. However, it was severely weakened in what had been two of the sport's strongest areas. From 22 clubs that originally split in 1895, within three years, 98 were affiliated to the NU. In the county championship, Yorkshire were not winners for 30 years, and Lancashire for more than 40. The RFU's club membership fell from 481 in 1893 to 244 in 1902. And England, lacking players from the prominent clubs in Yorkshire and Lancashire, did not win the international championship for nearly 20 years.

2. Our Friends in the North

Spring 1995

It had been a rugby league season much like any other in recent years. Wigan continued to be the team to beat. With the Regal Trophy already safely housed at Central Park, and still very much in the hunt for the other three major domestic titles, they looked favourites to continue their domination of the English game. While Wigan were quite rightly generating positive headlines for some superlative play there was still plenty of negative publicity finding its way into the media. Despite all the supposed improvements in relations made over the years at junior level, the majority of rugby union's restrictions remained in force, affecting anyone who turned out for a professional league club. As the weeks ticked by towards the spring the latest, and as it would prove the last Welsh international convert, Scott Quinnell was showing increasingly promising signs of learning his new league trade at Wigan. Meanwhile another, Stuart Evans, was campaigning very publicly for reinstatement into union now that his professional contract had ended without being forced to serve a three year stand down period. Enforced idleness in rugby union was the prospect for one young northern student, Adrian Spencer, who was kicking his heels at Cambridge University now that his 12 month ban for playing as an amateur in rugby league with London Crusaders had taken effect.

These three were probably the most notable names who made the headlines that season for finding themselves at odds with the world of rugby union – the latest individuals to find themselves embroiled in a battle that had been running for so long that it was practically woven into the traditions of both games. For a league fan it was a depressingly unchanging, unjust situation with apparently no imminent end in sight. Still, as the season drew towards its close all league fans could look forward to the Cup Final weekend when, hopefully, the game would once again rise to the occasion and answer its critics in the best way possible, on the field of play.

That seemingly traditional spring was to be thrown abruptly into turmoil as the commercial fallout from the intense competition developing around the domestic pay-television market spread beyond Australia's borders. After failing in its bid to grab the television rights for the Winfield Cup from Kerry Packer, Rupert Murdoch's Newscorp announced the launch of a rival competition, the Star League at the start of April. To further his aims, Murdoch approached the Rugby Football League (RFL) in England with a deal that they quickly understood could not be refused. By the end of April 1995, Newscorp held the broadcast rights and virtual operational control over European Rugby League and the embryonic Star League in the southern hemisphere.

As the rugby league world came to terms with the implications of Murdoch's global ambitions, he himself was off in pursuit of new quarry. This time the target was rugby union and on 23 June, the eve of the World Cup Final in Johannesburg, executives of Newscorp announced they had secured the rights to show a range of representative matches under the control of the Australian, New Zealand and South African (SANZA) Unions for the next ten years. Determined to hurt his league rival in his new venture, Kerry Packer funded a short-lived alternative union body to contract SANZA's star names with the intention of denying them to Murdoch's channels.

When news of the SANZA deal came to the attention of Peter Higham, the Chairman of Warrington RLFC, he was quoted as saying: "I envisage only one code of rugby by the turn of the century, and this Murdoch deal will be the stepping stone on the way."

Higham's scenario was not that far fetched as articles were appearing in the Australian press claiming that definite plans were already in place to bring about reunification.

While the leaguers speculated about plots for reunification, those involved with union had other fears. What if Newscorp did not get the viewers to cover its huge investment? Would they have the power to force one or both games to make law changes to attract more viewers and if so would they exercise it?

Alarm bells began to sound in the offices of the European Rugby Unions as the implications of Murdoch and Packer's activities in the southern hemisphere became clear to them – the sums of money and time involved meant the leading players could no longer be considered as amateur; they would have to be professionals. After a century of shoring up, this time there was no doubt that the wind of change blowing from the south was going to demolish the ancient, rickety structure of amateurism that the British Home Unions had held so dear. Rugby union's global governing body, the International Rugby Board (IRB), met in a Paris hotel over the weekend of 26 and 27 August to work out what could be done. Eventually those present came to the realisation nothing more was possible and without even taking a vote decided to repeal the amateur regulations and declare rugby union an open game – paving the way for today's full-time professionalism at the top level and part-time professionalism lower down.

Where arguments about individual rights and even appeals for fair play had failed for so long, a rapid corporate intervention backed by sufficient cash had won the day. Despite attempts to hold back the introduction in England for 12 months, the world of rugby union was effectively open almost 100 years to the day after the game's then leaders had turned their backs on such base commercial considerations. Throughout those intervening years the future of rugby had been very much dependent on its past. What would its future be in this brave new world?

The original sin

An understanding of what it meant for rugby union to go open has to begin with the build up to the original split, one of the most documented and hotly debated events in English sporting history. Back in the spring of 1895, a group of Northern clubs were approaching the end of their third season of organised league competition in the Yorkshire Senior Competition and the First Division of the Lancashire Club Championship. To improve their competitive position, those clubs devised a plan to spread beyond their county boundaries and create a new body, the Lancashire and Yorkshire Rugby Union of Senior Clubs that could match the Football League. Unfortunately, the Rugby Football Union (RFU) rejected this proposal as prejudicial to the interests of the game in May 1895, forcing those senior clubs to take stock of their situation.

Once it became clear to them that the RFU was planning to introduce even more stringent amateur regulations later that year, those senior clubs had to face up to some hard choices. Over the close season the debate raged – a small minority arguing to stay with the RFU and fight their case. The majority determined that rather than be picked off individually they would leave as a group and create their own independent elite union.

On the evening of Thursday 29 August, 21 senior clubs met at Huddersfield to determine the course they would take. Eventually 20 of those present agreed that they would submit their resignations to the RFU and form a new Northern Union (NU). Two clubs from Cheshire applied immediately and were accepted into membership. To meet the needs of its members, a Northern Rugby League (NRL), comprising all 22 clubs, was formed to harness their competitive ambitions. To cope with the increased travel distances on match days, expense payments for leaving work early, known as 'broken-time', were approved. These payments were fixed at 6/- (£0.30) per day with only one day being payable in relation to any match. Such payments had been rejected two years earlier by the RFU as being contrary to their amateur regulations.

Subsequently all those involved in the Northern Union, having agreed to pay 'broken-time' were declared professional. It did not matter whether they had accepted broken-time payments or not they were still professionalised and therefore could have no contact with anyone involved in amateur rugby union. As the rebels drew up their own NRL programme the impending rugby union season was thrown into chaos as many clubs had to reorganise their fixture lists. Over the last three weeks of the close season the die was cast. The RFU ruled that no matches with the rebel clubs were to be permitted; no players would be allowed to

11

participate in matches under the control of the rebel union and even more restrictively placed the rebels' grounds out of bounds for all fixtures.

In quick succession the other three Home Unions lined up behind the RFU, which precluded them or the IRB from actively mediating in the short-term. Tarred with the original sin of professionalism, the rebels were left to their own devices. What the rebels had to their advantage was a strong belief that their proposals were essential if the rugby game wanted to prosper. So widespread was that belief that over the next five years the vast majority of the clubs – junior and senior – in the northern counties of England switched over to the rebel union.

An unequal reaction

Affronted by the Northern defection, the RFU's leadership launched a fierce and unyielding battle for the game's soul. Professionalism, legalised years earlier, had helped transform association football from a kick-and-chase affair into a fast, spectacular, skilful game devoid of much of its roughness. Through their efforts the game had grown in popularity and the professionals had quite rightly grown in stature. A similar process would occur in the world of rugby union a century later, but in 1895 the RFU was determined to deny the professionals the chance to play any leading role.

Ever since association football had allowed professionalism, a number of leading members of the RFU had been openly discussing what would be the implications of a similar process occurring in rugby. Arthur Budd a former member of the RFU Committee spelt out his view in 1892 of the dire consequences facing that body if such an event was to happen. For Budd, the professionals would seize the initiative for "... a man who gives his whole time to a game is bound to best the amateur, who devotes only his leisure to it ... and it simply becomes a question of how long the amateur can survive."

In the aftermath of the Northern Union's exit, Arthur Budd was quick to depict publicly the split as advantageous. Writing in 1897, Budd saw the situation quite simply: "There has been a fairly large exodus of clubs to join the Northern Union. ... Though we are fewer in numbers than we were, I think we can congratulate ourselves that we are in a very much healthier condition, and that in purifying our ranks we now have the assistance of the Northern Union, who have proved themselves to be a most admirable drainage pipe."

For Budd and the many others who thought like him there was great relief that the professional pressure had been eased.

Once prised apart, the amateurs would publicly credit themselves with maintaining a game purely for the benefit of the players, although this in practice meant mostly carrying on playing an unchanging game. Meanwhile it was predicted that the professionals would set about

12

creating a new version of the rugby game that was more spectator-friendly. Being professionals, that approach was only to be expected as without the spectators there would be no revenue to fund the Northern Union's future development. However, the fact they did include the spectators' interests in their deliberations was used unmercifully by their opponents to denigrate every change made as being tainted by purely commercial intentions. As was to be expected while Budd's ideas were in the ascendancy, all the Northern Union's innovations were shunned as it was considered they would probably make the game too demanding and certainly less enjoyable for the amateurs.

To restrict the Northern Union's influence spreading outside the north of England, the RFU leadership made it clear it was prepared to sacrifice any of its own who showed any sympathy if necessary. Anyone considering following the rebel path had to face up to a stark choice – leaving the RFU carried with it a life sentence. There must be no contact and no succour; individuals, clubs and grounds were placed beyond the pale. As a result, families were split, father pitted against son, brother against brother in a battle driven by a moral fervour that would quite happily consign anyone who opposed the RFU's stance to the rugby equivalent of eternal damnation. Whereas the leadership of other overseas Unions would in later years show some leniency by regularly, if selectively, allowing reinstatement, the RFU would never offer any such hope to former professionals. This position was tempered somewhat in Wales where reinstatement was used as a way of undermining any attempt to launch junior rugby league in that country.

After all, what interest could the RFU have in a returning professional? They were dangerous men who had worked against the interests of the leading amateur players and had dallied with subversive ideas of what the game was all about. No matter what it did, the Northern Union had no way of closing the distance between itself and the RFU. It would have been understandable had the rising levels of bitterness led it into pointless acts of retaliation, but the Northern Union managed to steer clear of most of those temptations and where possible assist all sections of amateur rugby if requested to do so.

With the benefit of a century's hindsight, it is easy now to believe that the RFU leadership acted in a manner out of all proportion with the small number of professionals that the original rebellion would have created. What was surprising was the willingness of subsequent generations of the RFU's leadership to deny reality and cling to Budd's legacy no matter how absurd its stance became. However, that same leadership was pragmatic enough to ditch that legacy and adopt a far different approach to the Northern Union in its heartland compared to that taken in the rest of England. Unfortunately, the British sporting public's perception of the battle between the two games was formed by what they saw happening in the country at large, largely because if at all possible it was denied any real knowledge of what was happening in those northern counties.

Old habits

For the RFU's leadership, September 1995 was a testing time fraught with difficulty with many adjustments being needed almost immediately from a group of men who had probably been more committed in their allegiance to the spirit of amateurism than any other. Suddenly that group had to embrace a whole new ethos and determine what kind of relationships they would establish in the new professional world, in particular, with their old adversary the RFL.

Overseas the rules had been applied far more leniently and those Unions that had been pushing the limits of the old amateur regulations were felt to be in the best position to make the most of the new era. Of those countries, it was generally agreed that Australia had been setting the pace and it was from there that the most immediate opportunities could be assessed. It had been known for quite a few years that the Australian RU was happy to permit the sort of things that had appeared to have helped force the game open, such as finding ways of rewarding its leading players, allowing former professionals to play whether the IRB agreed or not, hiring rugby league grounds for major matches and seeking the assistance of rugby league coaches. Other countries such as France had also followed a similar path, but in England the RFU had very publicly refused to countenance such innovations.

If it was the fault of all or just some of those innovations then the game should have gone open many years before. While there is no evidence of illicit reinstatement when it came to the hiring of rugby league grounds for matches, major or otherwise and the use of ex-professionals as club coaches the RFU had quite a colourful past that it seemed to want to forget. When the union game went open great importance was attached to maintaining the notion that relations with the rugby league game had been permanently frozen for the past century. In reality the RFU had been very good at condoning what the Australians were up to many years earlier in the north of England.

While the split was still a very recent memory, the RFU had to face up to the question of its relations with the Northern Union if it was to retain any presence in the north of England. It needed to generate some publicity and what better way could there be to achieve that than through the staging of some big matches at major grounds. Unfortunately, nearly all the latter were beyond their control. Being aware that any approach would be accommodated by the Northern Union clubs if at all possible, the possibility of ground use was raised with the RFU Committee. Common sense appeared to prevail and the RFU responded in late August 1902 to Wakefield RUFC that its proposed match against another new club, Wakefield Balne Lane at Belle Vue, the home of Wakefield Trinity on Boxing Day could go ahead. A major factor in swaying the Committee apparently was the ownership of the ground and that no money taken at rugby union matches would find its way to the Northern Union Club. Technically Trinity were only tenants at Belle Vue, the ground being owned by the nominally independent Wakefield Trinity Athletic Company. At a stroke, rugby unionists no longer need fear stepping on to Belle Vue – it was effectively common ground when it was hired by a respectable rugby union organisation. The match duly went ahead on Boxing Day in front of a large crowd.

The implications of this sensible use of existing resources were not lost on the RFU's local officialdom. During 1903 Belle Vue hosted successfully a Yorkshire Rugby Union Cup Final replay and then less successfully the Roses County match. There was nothing restricting such matches to Belle Vue and soon the possibilities of other more central grounds were being considered for hire. When the 'original' All Blacks arrived in 1905, the Yorkshire RU was almost spoilt for choice receiving offers of four grounds, all free of charge. After initially agreeing to stage the match at the Boulevard, Hull, the match was subsequently switched to Headingley. That decision to switch grounds was vindicated when a crowd of 23,683 turned out on a December Wednesday afternoon, an unprecedented figure for a rugby union fixture in the North since the split. This figure would remain unbeaten for nearly 90 years.

This beneficial arrangement was repeated with Yorkshire's match against the first Springboks being played at Headingley and against the first Wallabies at Belle Vue. For these matches attendances fell sharply from that phenomenal turn out for the All Blacks and reined in some of the more fanciful ideas amongst the rugby unionists about regaining their former standing. In addition to these representative fixtures, grounds such as Belle Vue and Fartown, the home of Huddersfield, were made available to the local rugby union club for Yorkshire Cup ties when they were drawn against attractive opposition.

If anything, the generosity of the Northern Union venues was even greater immediately after the Great War. After nearly five seasons of inactivity, many new and existing rugby union clubs had to find new grounds. To try and help their struggling neighbours, Huddersfield twice made Fartown available to the local Old Boys in December 1920 and January 1921 to help them raise money for a new grandstand. The fans responded to the cause around 11,000 attending the two matches; many more than would have normally watched Old Boys in an entire season. Keighley similarly made Lawkholme Lane available "out of true sporting spirit" or in other words free of charge to their new neighbours, Keighlians, for a Yorkshire Rugby Union Cup tie in February 1922. Ground loans became so regular in some districts that the local media judged them hardly newsworthy.

Not everyone involved in league was always happy with such arrangements. When Hull allowed Hull and East Riding to use the Boulevard for a Yorkshire RU Cup tie at the end of February 1925 they did so in the knowledge that it clashed with a Hull KR home league fixture. Rovers were not at all pleased and appealed to the RFL to prevent it, but that was beyond their powers. Both matches went ahead and a 5,000 crowd attended the union game, but that was not to be the end of the matter. It was raised at the League's AGM where it was agreed that in future the Rugby League Council would have the power to prevent any match being held on the ground of a member if it could be shown to be against the interests of another. The powers do not ever appear to have been used and the practice continued throughout the inter-war years.

Having forcibly excluded so many experienced men from their ranks, the RFU found itself short of former players who 'understood' the game sufficiently to harness the raw talent of the young men who had the chance to take up the game after the First World War. A lucky few had taken advantage of their time serving the colours to play alongside professionals and learn new skills. One of them was a young pilot by the name of Wavell Wakefield, who was destined to become one of England rugby union's greatest forwards and later one of its most eminent administrators. Writing nearly 10 years later in his book *Rugger*, Wakefield expressed his gratitude to Lieutenant Billy Seddon, formerly with Wigan NUFC for teaching him "... the secret of spin-kicking". Wakefield also praised Seddon's play, describing him as "...a very fine kick himself, (who) won more than one match for us with his long-range dropped goals". Why shouldn't rugby union clubs turn to former professionals to take on a similar role in peace? Obviously the ex-professionals could not openly describe themselves as coaches; that would have been against both the spirit and the letter of the law. However, the laws allowed for them to be paid a nominal amount as a baggage man or general attendant and that was how they were known.

Even 40 years on, many rugby union club officials were still embarrassed by what their forebears had done to meet their need for quality coaching. During the 1920s a number of retired leading players were very happy to take on this role and quite publicly too as their proud appearance on team group photographs show. Ben Gronow, a Welsh RU International before touring Australasia with the Northern Union in 1920 and 1924 and one of rugby league's most famous forwards, did the job for Morley RUFC and later Huddersfield Old Boys RUFC. Herbert Kershaw after a successful 15 year career with Trinity returned to his old club, Wakefield RUFC, at the end of the 1920s and gave them over 10 years service. One of Kershaw's team mates on the 1910 Northern Union tour was Joe Riley who after similarly long service at Thrum Hall moved across town to Ovenden Park where he coached the newly formed Halifax RUFC for many years. Between those three coaches some very successful teams were produced, which contained the first players to gain England 'caps' from their clubs since the split.

Using former rugby league players as coaches was most prevalent in Yorkshire, but it was also to be found in Lancashire. After the First World War George Marsden, a dual international previously with Morley RUFC and Bradford Northern, took up residence in Lytham St Anne's where he assisted with the formation of Fylde RUFC in 1919. Without his expertise it would have been much more difficult to knock into shape the club's initial recruits – Fylde's Jubilee history records that few of its founders had seen a rugby union match before let alone played in one. Many other less famous players were to be found holding similar positions with both senior and junior clubs in Lancashire and Yorkshire.

Besides coaching there were other public displays of support, many involving the offspring of ex-professionals. A very prominent case was Harold Wagstaff, one of league's legendary figures and a founder member of the Hall of Fame, whose contributions to Huddersfield Old Boys activities increased as his son Bob made his breakthrough into that Club's first team in the late 1930s. He appeared in the Old Boys monthly lecture programme, which were always well attended and his tactical advice was sought regularly before important matches and cup ties.

Although attempts to resume previous arrangements were made after the Second World War, there was little time before the RFU intervened. In late June 1948 the RFU and WRU agreed to reinstate the original view on league grounds – that ownership was not the ultimate determinant. Once more a ground was to be placed out of bounds if it was the regular home of a rugby league club. For the record, the last major fixture to be completed before this ban took effect was held at Belle Vue Zoological Gardens, the home of Belle Vue Rangers where a combined Lancashire and Cheshire XV secured a famous victory over the Third Wallabies in front of a 15,000 crowd. At the same time the RFU included extra laws to prohibit the use of former professionals as coaches.

Stadium usage being so visible it was a prohibition that could not easily be circumvented. It was a different story when it came to coaches, who really could operate like invisible men and their presence was never completely eradicated. Former professionals, well known in their own locality were still approached and accepted those positions – amongst them Don Gullick, formerly of St Helens at West Park, Fred Rule, formerly of Halifax at Halifax RUFC, George Todd, formerly of Halifax at Roundhay, George Brown, formerly of Batley at Morley and Alex Fiddes and Dave Valentine, who both went from Fartown to Huddersfield RUFC.

The end of this long and honourable line effectively came with the hounding of Ray French. As time went on his titular position as a local liaison officer with St Helens RUFC provided less and less cover and following an investigation by the Lancashire RU during 1975-76 he was

Ben Gronow - one of the most famous rugby league players of his generation.
(Photo: Courtesy Robert Gate)

Two rugby league legends:

Left: Harold Wagstaff

Below: Dave Valentine

(Photos: Courtesy Robert Gate)

19

forced to resign as coach. Over on the other side of the Pennines, Johnny Whiteley, the former Hull FC rugby league international loose-forward and coach of Great Britain, was forced out of a coaching role with a Hull junior rugby union club. A few others were ejected that same season. Many of those coaches had built excellent records, successfully developing rugby union players imbued with a strong element of individual league skills and tactics. They could and did produce teams that played in a hybrid style that often drew compliments from observers when they ventured outside the North.

Across the northern counties there were plenty of positive experiences, whether from coaching or from ground use that could have been built upon, but hardly anyone on the RFU leadership, even during the inter-war years, ever wanted to know. Even then, there had been no contact on the field of play. It required an even greater hostility than that to be found in the world of rugby to create a situation where that could come about.

A higher authority

When English rugby union went open there were many people vaguely aware that years earlier there had been a section of the game where a semblance of a working relationship had been possible, and that was in the armed forces. Although that situation had only existed at times of national emergency, it had created the possibility for the military to show the grassroots of the rugby game that some form of unity could be brought about. With the nation mobilised to face a dire threat, the sporting background of young men, especially conscripts, paled into insignificance and they could be treated simply as rugby players. As far as the RFU was concerned, this situation would only last while the battle raged. When it ended their authority would be reasserted and a narrow amateurism would rule once more.

For the first 18 months of the First World War, there was little sign of cooperation until the introduction of conscription and the Northern Union's suspension of professionalism provided a basis for the two rugby games to rediscover some common ground at the start of 1916. At a local level the two games began to find ways they could cooperate, at least by promoting matches designed to support some aspect of the war effort while also providing some sporting entertainment for those at home.

Bob Oakes, the treasurer of Yorkshire RU, with the approval of Northern Command at Catterick raised teams, which assumed the title of the Northern Military XV, to play a series of matches in the spring of 1916. These matches, which generated great enthusiasm amongst players and spectators alike, provided the first occasion since the split for rugby union and Northern Union players to take the field together. Four leading players who had appeared in the Northern Union test team, all members of Huddersfield's hugely successful 'Team of all the Talents', – captain and centre Harold

Wagstaff, half-back Johnny Rogers, and forwards Douglas Clark and Ben Gronow – were featured in the side. Alongside them in those Northern military sides were fellow test centre and former Welsh rugby union international, Willie A. Davies (Leeds), and the uncapped full-back Billy Seddon (Wigan).

The first match was held at Headingley on Saturday 8 April 1916 where Oakes' team beat the Australasian Forces 13-11 in front of 10,000 spectators. Four former Kangaroos – Viv Farnsworth (Oldham), Tommy Gleeson (Huddersfield), and Jim Devereux and Sid Deane (Hull) – played for the Australasian Forces. It was a show of unity many were waiting for and immediately afterwards the former Hull captain C.C. Lempriere wrote to *The Yorkshire Post* calling attention to the opportunity the match had provided for reuniting the game. Three weeks later on Saturday 29 April, Oakes took his team to the Victoria Ground, Hartlepool, the home of Hartlepool United to meet a Tees and Hartlepool Garrison XV. It provided a town that was a great nursery of rugby talent with a rare chance to watch Northern Union players in action. Finally on Saturday 20 May 1916 an Oakes XV met a Welsh XV at Anfield, the home of Liverpool F.C. The Welsh team, which was composed entirely of men in essential work, was raised by Captain Walter Rees, the secretary of the Welsh RU. A crowd estimated somewhere between 15,000 and 20,000 watched the match.

As a result of Oakes' activities and his representations the RFU and the Welsh RU agreed to suspend the professional laws as they applied to men in uniform for the duration of the war. The RFU issued the following statement on 4 October 1916, supposedly clarifying the position as far as Northern Union players were concerned.

"Northern Union players can only play with rugby union players in bona-fide Naval and Military teams. rugby union teams can play against Naval and Military teams in which there are Northern Union players. Munitions workers cannot be regarded as Naval and Military players. These rulings only apply during the war."

The RFU's minimal approval appears to have been widely disregarded at the civilian grassroots of the game and even within the military.

One of the leading military teams was just being assembled when the RFU issued its statement. It was the brainchild of Robert V. Stanley, a Major serving with the Motor Transport Army Service Corps (A.S.C.) based at Grove Park in north-west London. Stanley enjoyed a high profile within the RFU, representing Oxford University on the RFU Committee and being appointed an England selector in 1913-14. Recognising the benefits brought by the Service matches organised by the Barbarians and Bob Oakes, Stanley assumed for himself and his unit the task of providing similar top-class rugby union in the Home Counties. Through his many connections his unit was able to obtain the services of many rugby union and Northern Union internationals and also to arrange an extensive fixture list. Led by Malcolm Neale, the former Bristol and England RU international, Stanley's team broke down barriers by fielding five leading members of Huddersfield NUFC – three of whom, Douglas Clark, Ben Gronow and Harold Wagstaff, had appeared for Oakes, plus Albert Rosenfeld (Australia) and Bill Trevarthen (New Zealand). Not surprisingly, their play had a major impact on the rugby union game in the Home Counties in 1916-17.

Between September 1916 and January 1917, the A.S.C. had played 18 matches, winning 17 against the likes of the Royal Engineers, a Public School Services XV, the Royal Flying Corps and the Manchester Regiment, scoring 907 points while conceding only 32. While some viewed the A.S.C. as one of the strongest sides ever seen in the capital, others pointed out correctly that a fair proportion of their opponents were scratch sides including convalescents, public schoolboys and a goodly number of average club players. Keen to see the A.S.C. matched against worthy opponents, a Scot, Dr J. A. Russell-Cargill assembled a strong United Services' team and arranged to use the Rectory Field at Blackheath. At the final whistle A.S.C. had suffered its first defeat, 6-3, largely as a result of the Services pack gaining the upper hand. The A.S.C. later won a return match against United Services 17-5.

What irked the A.S.C.'s critics was the way the team demonstrated the advantages of the modern professional approach. In the professional game the pack was expected to be involved in far more than just scrummaging. Rather than expend lots of their strength trying to make ground in shoving contests, the professionals bound far looser and broke up faster, which led to them being described by some rugby union traditionalists as little more than hooking and heeling machines. While Stanley had his A.S.C. team together in the capital, they both challenged and undermined in many metropolitan eyes the old style rough, shoving rugby that had been the original product of the public schools.

In a review of the season's play, it was recorded in *The Tatler* on 28 March 1917 that the A.S.C. had played and won 21 of their 22 matches scoring 1,046 points whilst only conceding 27. Single-handedly Ben Gronow had contributed 106 goals and 20 tries to that points total. That same article rated two products of the Northern Union's junior ranks, Harold Wagstaff and Douglas Clark respectively, as the best back and one of the best forwards seen in wartime matches. Sadly it proved impossible for the A.S.C. to arrange a match with either the Welsh XV or the R.N. Depot team from Devonport up to that point. Most of the A.S.C.'s matches had been played at Rosslyn Park's ground at Richmond's Old Deer Park and drawn sufficiently good crowds for the organisers to report a balance in hand of £617 at the end of the 1916-17 season. That review contributed greatly to the break up of the A.S.C. team; within weeks the players received their postings.

While the Northern Union had appreciated the accolades bestowed on the A.S.C., a greater impact on the rugby game in the north of England resulted from visits by a Service team based in faraway Devon. The Royal Navy Depot team, which drew on all Service personnel based at Devonport depot, was organised by Warrant Writer T. J. Buckley and proved a prominent force in wartime sport. Matches were organised against Cardiff, Swansea, Monmouthshire, Western Counties, Leicester, Gloucester, Cross Keys and Llanelli. Representative teams were welcomed with matches being staged at Plymouth Argyle FC's ground, Home Park. However, it was the Depot's ground-breaking decision to play matches against various Northern Union club sides that proved most significant. Under the captaincy of Willie A. Davies, the undefeated R.N. Depot team gained permission to play a charity match, similar to those arranged by Oakes against his old club. The sailors' visit aroused great enthusiasm and they beat Leeds on Saturday 24 March 1917 at Headingley 19-13 under rugby union rules. In defeat, the Leeds team was far from disgraced, having coped well with a set of very fit opponents and the alien rules, which exposed just how ignorant many of them were with regard to the technicalities of the union game. At the after match function, hopes were expressed that other fixtures might be arranged and the Leeds club was promised a warm welcome should it be able to make a visit to Plymouth.

Although rail transport was difficult to obtain, that did not prevent a once again undefeated R.N. Depot undertaking a northern tour over Christmas 1917. Willie Davies again secured a fixture with Leeds and Jack Beames, Halifax's Welsh forward then serving with the Navy, made a similar arrangement with his old Club. Besides those two fixtures the Depot also scheduled matches with Wigan on 22 December and Hull on Boxing Day when it was hoped that the R.N. Depot team would include several Hull K.R. players. Unfortunately both those matches fell victim to frost and had to be cancelled. There was more success with the other two fixtures, the first on Christmas Eve when a strengthened Leeds were beaten 9-3. The following day they faced Halifax, where despite the home side borrowing both Jack Beames and Cyril Stacey from the Depot squad, the visitors won 26-12. To make up for the earlier disappointments, an extra match was arranged with Leeds on 28 December. This match, played 13-a-side under rugby union laws was probably as near to a cross-code challenge as an ostensibly loyal senior rugby union team could get without flouting all convention. Once again the Depot proved superior running out comfortable winners 24-3.

Even though the War was over and men were beginning to be discharged, a depleted Depot team returned to Yorkshire over Christmas 1918 and suffered two defeats at the hands of Halifax NUFC separated by a nil-nil draw at Batley NUFC on Boxing Day. After that the Depot team travelled homewards and all contact between the two games ceased. Peace lasted for 20 years and while it did there would be no matches where the two rugby games could get together. Unfortunately, peace proved short-lived as Hitler and the other dictators rose to power on the back of the First World War's unresolved issues. What had once been thought unthinkable, a new war, finally broke out at the start of September 1939 and recreated some of the old camaraderie.

With conscription already on the statute books, the way was clear for the two rugby games to co-operate immediately. Probably the first to cross the divide was Huddersfield RLFC, which finding it had a blank Saturday in mid-October issued a challenge for any opponents to present themselves. That challenge was accepted by the local Anti-Aircraft detachment and a match under rugby union rules was arranged for 14 October. Just over two months into the conflict, on 12 November 1939, the RFU passed a resolution allowing rugby league players in the Armed Forces, who had had no association with rugby league since their enlistment, to participate in union matches between clubs and service teams for the duration of the war. That resolution accepted that:

a. A Rugby XV may play against a Service XV containing players who have played Rugby league football.
b. A Rugby Union XV may include Rugby League players belonging to His Majesty's Forces when playing matches against Service teams.
c. A Rugby Union XV may include Rugby League players belonging to the Forces when playing against another Rugby Union club.

As in the previous conflict, the Welsh RU followed the RFU's lead whereas the Scottish RU insisted that the ban on rugby league players taking part in any match against a team under its jurisdiction must remain in force.

Facing the gravest threat imaginable, it was a time to end old divisions, to close ranks and present a united front to the enemy. Those sentiments spread throughout society and the two rugby games once again drew together in England and Wales. Central Park, Wigan demonstrated just what could be achieved in those circumstances with goodwill on both sides. Then a major coal mining centre, Wigan had a large number of men in reserved occupations and these enabled the town's rugby league club to remain active through all six wartime seasons. Besides the league fixtures it also hosted major charity rugby Union fixtures and a number of Service matches featuring the RAF and the Combined Services. It was also used quite regularly for matches by a number of rugby union clubs. One of those matches provided Jim Sullivan of Wigan RLFC with a chance to play once again his old game for Wigan Old Boys. In both March 1941 and March 1942, Central Park was made available without charge for matches between teams titled Lancashire RU and Yorkshire RU, the proceeds going to the British Red Cross.

Once again Services' rugby union expanded dramatically. Whether training, waiting to be deployed or on active service in one of the many different theatres of war, there was a great deal of enthusiasm amongst servicemen for a game of rugby. Inter-unit and regimental matches flourished and both the Army and the RAF managed to field fully representative teams on a regular basis. This presented the RFL with a major problem and the secretary approached the Service rugby unions to

Second World War rugby union services international: Wales versus England at Swansea. Rugby union star Haydn Tanner passing, with rugby league star Trevor Foster on his left. (Photo: Courtesy Simon Foster)

try and ensure that a balance was struck was struck that did not affect adversely the wartime league matches. Although transport continued to be a major headache for fixture organisers, the problems had eased sufficiently for a programme of wartime rugby union internationals to begin during 1941-42 under the auspices of the Inter-Services Committee. Those Service internationals as they were known created great public interest as well as healthy proceeds for Service charities. For many sportsmen the war not only threatened to end their lives, but the possibility they may have had of a successful sporting career. Those unofficial international matches played a valuable role in providing, at least for some prominent servicemen billeted in Britain, the opportunity to represent their country in a uniform other than worsted.

England played 16 matches against Scotland and Wales – the latter two countries only eight as they never arranged to meet each other. A number of serving rugby league players, many of whom were pre-war internationals, were selected to appear alongside various past and future internationals for the English and Welsh sides. Despite their hostility to the whole idea, Scotland did agree to meet English teams containing league men. The Scots even allowed some professionals to set foot on

Murrayfield's previously unsullied turf once it was released from its role as a supply depot by the War Department. Suddenly a host of professionalized players with a strong union background were made available to the Welsh team, their English equivalents having had in most cases only a brief flirtation with the union game. For the record the English Services included seven professional rugby league backs – Stan Brogden (Hull), Roy Francis (Barrow), Albert Johnson (Warrington), Johnny Lawrenson (Wigan), Harold Pimblett (St Helens), Jimmy Stott (St Helens) and Ernest Ward (Bradford Northern). Some strange military logic must have been at work to push a few Welshmen into those English teams, but once done it could not be undone and Roy Francis just had to accept the decision and make the best of his time as an England threequarter. Only four professionals found their way into the English pack – Ted Bedford (Hull K.R.), Ned Hodgson (Broughton Rangers), Ken Jubb (Leeds), and Ted Sadler (Castleford). While one or two of the professionals chosen had some junior experience only the English International Ted Sadler had previously gained senior representative rugby union honours.

In every international the Welsh Services proved to be a very effective combination; their outstanding backs enabling them to record seven victories over England from their eight meetings. So total was the integration that Gus Risman of Salford was even accorded the honour of captaining the team when his commitments to the First Airborne Regiment permitted. In addition to Risman the following backs made appearances for Wales – Alban Davies (Huddersfield), D. Idwal Davies (Leeds), Billy Davies (Bradford Northern), Alan Edwards (Salford), Cliff Evans (Leeds), Randell Lewis (Swinton), and Syd Williams (Salford). Included in the Welsh pack were Emrys Evans (Salford), Trevor Foster (Bradford Northern), Ike Owens (Leeds), Doug Phillips (Oldham), Jim Regan (Huddersfield), Harold Thomas (Salford), Eddie Watkins (Wigan) and Gwyn Williams (Wigan).

It had been Gwyn Williams's wish that one day he would be able to appear in a Service international alongside his highly rated younger brother Bleddyn. That wish appeared to be coming true when Bleddyn was chosen to make his debut alongside Gwyn against England at Gloucester on 20 March 1943. Sadly before the day of the match, Gwyn was posted to North Africa where he suffered such severe wounds that he never played again. In his absence, Bleddyn began his representative career that day with a hat-trick of tries and proceeded to enjoy a long and successful peace-time career. For the hugely promising 20-year-old Aircraftsman, the chance to play centre alongside the likes of Billy Davies and Gus Risman provided an invaluable learning experience. Williams later recalled those experiences in a piece he contributed to Gloucester RUFC's book celebrating *125 Glorious Years:* "There was no acrimony and I have not the slightest hesitation in saying that those games, in which I was

26

extremely privileged to take part for three years, produced some of the most exhilarating and spectacular rugger of my day."

There was another family reconnection as a result of those matches – Billy Davies was allowed the chance to resume his pre-war club and international half-back partnership with his cousin Haydn Tanner.

As Williams says, the Service internationals provided superb showcases for the players' combined skills and raised hopes that post-war rugby union would concentrate more on constructive attacking play rather than the spoiling that had been so prevalent in the 1930s. While some of England's international matches were staged in the provinces, at Gloucester and Leicester, none were held in the north.

Beyond those international matches, there were two events that particularly captured the attention of rugby enthusiasts in northern England. They were the two matches that pitted Service teams from rugby league and rugby union against each other. Even though both were held XV-a-side under rugby union rules with the proceeds going to war charities, they were not universally welcomed. After all they reminded the sporting world of the still close similarity of the two games and the absurdity of their separation.

Saturday 23 January 1943 – organised by the Army's Northern Command Sports Board at the Headingley Grounds, Leeds.
Rugby League XV (3) 18 Rugby Union XV (8) 11. Attendance: 8,000.

A luncheon was held prior to the match and it allowed a number of leading of figures involved with the game to air their views. The match organiser, Captain Stanley Wilson of the Army's Northern Command, expressed his personal sentiments when he called "... for the playing of an annual fixture between the union and the league in the hope of eventually healing the breach". Responding, Bob Oakes, the Yorkshire RU president, stressed that while the two games would probably go their own separate ways after the war there could be no line of demarcation between men in uniform. Once more he repeated his view that if a man was good enough to wear the King's uniform there should be no barrier to stop him playing any game he liked. John Wilson,

SOUVENIR PROGRAMME

NORTHERN COMMAND REPRESENTATIVE
RUGBY MATCH

(Under the patronage of Lt. Gen. Sir T. R. EASTWOOD,
K.C.B., D.S.O., M.C., G.O.C. in C. Northern Command)

UNION XV

VERSUS

LEAGUE XV

(Under Union Rules)

at

Leeds R.L. Football Club Ground

Headingley

(By kind permission of the Directors)

on

Saturday, January 23rd, 1943

Kick off 3-30 p.m.

ORGANISED BY THE NORTHERN COMMAND
SPORTS BOARD.

(Courtesy Robert Gate)

the secretary of the RFL, while regretting the past, tacitly agreed with Oakes, for "… in his view rugby would have been a better game had those who ruled it at the time of the split on professionalism taken the broader outlook of the officials of the Association code, (but) he did not think that the two rugby codes would ever come together and play under one banner".

While his expectations were obviously low, he did however keep his options partially open by saying that he saw no reason why such a match should not become an annual event. The union team's captain for this match, Captain N. M. Walford (Oxford University) expressed plainly his own personal sentiments, saying "… we are concerned solely with playing rugby and not whom we are playing with or against."

A close match was expected as half of the league's forwards were formerly Welsh union players. According to Ken Dalby, as a consequence of their adaptation to the play-the-ball rules, those Welshmen were disadvantaged in the rucks and obviously lacked practice at the line-out. At half-back, the League XV had problems in the first-half, kicking far too infrequently to touch in defence. This was only to be expected when it is realised that their scrum-half, Billy Thornton (Hunslet) was playing only his second game of union. Unfortunately for the Union XV, Cowe had to leave the field in the second-half and that provided the league team with sufficient advantage to secure victory. The match was played in a good spirit and the play was of a high enough quality to ensure that future meetings would draw good crowds. Dalby recognised that amongst the players there was something extra about this match, something more than a run-of-the-mill exhibition match, and it seemed to inspire the League XV to raise their game in the second-half and record a famous victory. The teams for the clash of the codes were:

League: Cpl G.R. Pepperell (Huddersfield); Sgt-I R.L. Francis (Dewsbury), Trpr H. Mills (Hull), Pte J. Stott (St. Helens), Cpl E.W. Lloyd (Castleford); L-Bdr H. Royal (Dewsbury), Sgm W. Thornton (Hunslet); Sgt-I D.R. Prosser (Leeds), L-Cpl L.L. White (Hunslet), Gnr L. White (York), Cpl K. Jubb (Leeds), Cpl E. Tattersfield (Leeds), Pte W. Chapman (Warrington), Cpl H. Bedford (Hull), Sgt-I T. Foster (Bradford Northern)

Union: Cpl J. Bond (Cumberland); Lt T.G.H. Jackson (Army), Capt N.M. Walford (Oxford University), Lt D.R. MacGregor (Rosslyn Park), Sgt-I D.F. Mitchell (Galashiels); 2nd-Lt L.B. Lockhart (Cambridge University), O-Cdt H. Tanner (Swansea); Major R.O. Murray (London Scottish), Sgm J.D.H. Hastie (Melrose), Cpl J. Maltman (Hawick), Cadet R.C.V. Stewart (Waterloo), Cpl R. Cowe (Melrose), 2nd-Lt R.A. Huskisson (Oxford University), Pte R.A. Crawford (Melrose), 2nd-Lt R.G. Furbank (Bedford).

However, a note of discord was struck on the day when details of a message received from the secretary of the Scottish RU were made public. The message raised concerns regarding Northern Command's next scheduled match against an Edinburgh University XV with the Scottish secretary demanding assurances from Northern Command that no member of their chosen team would have played rugby league. When no such assurance was forthcoming the fixture was cancelled.

Saturday 29 April 1944 – organised by the Inter-Service Rugby Football Committee at Odsal Stadium, Bradford.

Rugby League Combined Services 15 Rugby Union Combined Services 10. Attendance: 18,000.

As all sections of the home-based Armed Forces were eligible for this match the teams should have been stronger, but turned out weaker due to late withdrawals through injury. Many had hopes that this second match would go further than the first and give some clues as to how the two games might complement each other in the future. Writing in *The Observer* T. H. Evans-Baillie sounded almost sad that "The different virtues brought out by the codes of union and league were not, and it is doubtful if they ever could be, put to a decisive test at Odsal Stadium, Bradford".

After initially struggling to cope with the union pack's open dribbling play and conceding two early tries, the league team mounted a fight back and eventually brought the scores level. It was the skill and artistry of the league team's backs which in the end determined the outcome of a close match. With three minutes remaining the league men worked a memorable score for Brogden. According to Evans-Baillie "Fittingly enough the match ended in a movement which demonstrated the constant acceleration of well done league attacks".

Once again victory had gone to the league men. The teams were:

League: L-Cpl E. Ward (Bradford Northern); Sgt-I R.L. Francis (Barrow), Cpl J. Stott (St Helens), LAC J. Lawrenson (Wigan), Cpl A. Edwards (Salford); Sgt S. Brogden (Hull), Bdr H. Royal (Dewsbury); Sgt-I D.R. Prosser (Leeds), Dvr L. White (Hunslet), LAC C. Brereton (Halifax), Dvr D. Murphy (Bramley), Flt-Sgt E. Watkins (Wigan), Sgt I.A. Owens (Leeds), Sgt W. Chapman (Warrington), Sgt-I T. Foster (Bradford Northern).

Union: CSM I. Trott (Penarth); Lt G. Hollis (Sale), Cpl T. Sullivan (Swansea), Lt H. Tanner (Swansea), Sub-Lt E.S. Simpson (Bradford); Lt T. Gray (Heriot's F.P.), Sqdn-Ldr J. Parsons (Leicester); Cpl R.J. Longland (Northampton), Sgt G.T. Dancer (Bedford), Capt R.E. Prescott (Harlequins), Lt P.M. Walker (Gloucester), Cpl D.V. Phillips (Swansea), Capt G.D. Shaw (Galashiels), Capt J.A. Waters (Selkirk), Flt-Lt R.G. Weighell (Waterloo).

While rugby unionists might point to the limitations of their selected teams, rugby league's supporters could equally point out that their teams were playing under largely alien rules. For rugby league's supporters the outcome of the two matches provided a timely boost to morale and a public testament to the professional qualities of their players. The hopes that such matches might continue to be held soon foundered and they remained a testimony more to the game's spirit in wartime rather than to any profound desire to heal the breach in English rugby. Although much has been made of these matches over the years, sadly little that was constructive came from them.

The surrender of Germany and shortly afterwards Japan offered a tired population the prospect of a well earned period of peace. Unfortunately it turned out to be an edgy kind of peace as Allied unity disintegrated into a new conflict. To cope with the onset of the Cold War and the retreat from Empire, an increased military presence was needed and Clement Atlee's Government reluctantly agreed in May 1947 to retain conscription. As a result, legislation was passed requiring all the country's young men to spend 18 months, increased to two years once the Korean War began, serving His Majesty. National Service, as it was known, was to cover all young men between the ages of 18 and 26. A conscript could apply to defer his enlistment until he was older if he had a good reason, but most chose to join up at 18 and get it over and done with. The vast majority of those young men found themselves directed to the Army, the rest going almost totally to the RAF as the Royal Navy chose not to become reliant on conscripts.

An immediate post-war directive from the RFU precluding National Servicemen from playing rugby league after enlistment was deemed an unacceptable restriction on conscripts' rights and was amended by the updated laws on professionalism of 1948. That more liberal draft included the following stipulations:

c. A rugby union player is permitted whilst in HM Forces, to play for a Services team in a rugby league game but may not play for any civilian team.

d. A rugby league player is permitted whilst in HM Forces to play in a Rugby Union game for a team composed entirely of serving members of HM Forces against an English or Welsh Rugby Union team only.

e. A Rugby league player who has played under the above may continue to play Rugby League Football for other than a Service team but cannot play Rugby Union Football except for a Service team.

For a National Serviceman, there were plenty of possibilities provided he could get permission from his Commanding Officer to leave camp at the weekend to fulfil his contract with his professional club. In return, the Commanding Officer generally demanded a degree of compromise to ensure that the conscript was available for all the important Service fixtures. Negotiations were conducted generally in an atmosphere of goodwill and led to leading servicemen playing midweek for their units, and alternating Saturdays between major union and league fixtures. It was also true that getting a weekend pass to play in a league match was far more likely if the camp was located within the northern rugby league heartland.

Not surprisingly considering all the conscripts available from a rugby union background, Services rugby union was of a very high standard at the time. Although initially handicapped, many conscripts from a rugby league background proved able to adapt rapidly to the new game and were soon appearing regularly for service teams. It was made very obvious by the asterisk printed against their names in the match programmes that some found themselves selected to play in rugby union's Inter-Service Tournament. This tournament, which was frequently attended by royalty, pitted the full might of the three Service teams against each other in a round-robin format at Twickenham. A good proportion of the rugby league players who got the chance to play there were highly praised by the press on their performance. It meant that a highly promising young player like Gunner Ike Southward could in spring 1956 enjoy being the toast of the crowd at both Twickenham and Borough Park, Workington. Many others, in addition to those select few, appeared for their units and regiments such as the Royal Army Signals Corps, the Duke of Wellington's Regiment and the Royal Artillery without ever taking the field at Twickenham.

Of all those young leaguers who served their Majesties, Jack Broome, a strong running centre or stand-off was probably the highest achiever. Broome, a product of the West Bank junior club in Widnes, had made his debut for Wigan RLFC in 1948 and went on to make two appearances for the England rugby league side two years later. While a conscript, he not only appeared at Twickenham for the Army, but went one stage higher by gaining selection for the Combined Services XV that met the touring Springboks on Boxing Day 1951. He completed a remarkable double when less than four weeks later he was again to be found lining up against a touring team. However, on the second occasion the setting, the opponents and the rules were all different. Instead of Twickenham the venue was Stamford Bridge where, on Wednesday 23 January 1952, Broome appeared in the stand-off position for a British Empire Rugby League XIII against the New Zealand Kiwis.

With memories of the excellent hybrid rugby union teams that had graced the war years still strong, many senior officers were inspired to try and produce their own equivalents. For that to become a reality the best possible talent had to be obtained. The RAF Union history recalls how their secretary, Squadron Leader Neil Cameron, built strong links in the early 1950s with club secretaries of both games to get early warning of talented youngsters coming up for call up so that they might be persuaded to choose the light blue as their Service preference. He was not alone in this approach. An early leader in this field was Major Gordon Fraser, of the 1st Training Regiment, Royal Corps of Signals based at Catterick Camp in north Yorkshire. Fraser built strong links to clubs and schools and these enabled him to marshal some of the best young rugby talent available to the Army. Talent was chased wherever it could be identified and as in the case of one 18-year-old Welshman, Billy Boston, it was widely rumoured that outside influences were at work to secure his posting to Catterick in late 1952. Those rumours singled out Hunslet's secretary as the man who had tipped off Major Fraser about Boston's potential. If that was the case then it would certainly help explain why Hunslet had official permission to speak to Boston and received an invite to the dinner held after the Army Cup Final at Aldershot on Wednesday 11 March 1953.

No one watching can have left that Final with any doubts about Boston's potential as the young centre contributed six tries to a memorable Signals' victory. Hunslet may have had officialdom on their side, but by then news of the Signals' performances had attracted many more league scouts. Although operating without official sanction, a delegation from Wigan followed Boston as he went on leave to Cardiff and two days after the Final convinced him to turn professional. Wigan initially kept the deal secret, maybe until a somewhat disappointed Major Fraser had been won over. Finally, the deal could be revealed and Boston was given his first run out at Central Park in an 'A' team fixture on Saturday 21 November. Releases were approved by Major Fraser and Boston was able to make nine first team appearances for Wigan in addition to his appearances for the Signals before the end of the season.

Major Fraser demanded high standards of training and preparation from his young conscripts and they responded. Always a youthful side, harnessing the best of league's individual skills in the union environment, the Signals proved capable of winning the Yorkshire RU County Cup on two occasions – 1951-52 and 1953-54, and the Army Cup on five occasions – 1948-49, 1949-50, 1950-51, 1952-53 and 1953-54. That level of success led to a suspension from those competitions in 1954-55 while an investigation into the Signals' recruitment procedures was carried out. The unit was cleared although the advantages enjoyed by a training regiment compared to a regiment of the line were recognised and reviewed. Alongside the aforementioned Boston in the Signals' squad were the likes of Phil Jackson, Brian Gabbitas and Jimmy Dunn, all future leading players in rugby league plus Norman Hall, Russell Robbins, Phil Horrocks-Taylor and Reg Higgins all of whom had or went on to receive international rugby union honours.

The Signals never lost their appetite for league talent and very nearly secured one of the greatest players produced in the 1950s. They harboured hopes that a late entrant, the 20-year-old Alex Murphy, league's top scrum-half, would find himself assigned to the Army Signals

Corps. Unfortunately for the Army, before Murphy could catch the train he was successfully diverted by the RAF, which then posted him to Haydock, a far more convenient base for his home ground than Catterick. Aircraftsman Murphy had a whirlwind introduction to service life, playing union for the Technical Training Command on his second day in uniform. A few days later he received a weekend pass that allowed him to take his place in the St Helens team that defeated Swinton in the Lancashire Cup Final on 29 October 1960. Competition between the RAF and St Helens could just about be handled, but things got more complicated once Great Britain also required his services. The RAF co-operated with the RFL and Murphy was able to make a major contribution to Britain's victory over France at Bordeaux on 11 December 1960. But when the British selectors wanted to include him in their team to meet France at St Helens on Saturday 28 January 1961, they discovered that their plans clashed with those of the RAF union's officials who wanted him to play on the same day against Harlequins. A deal was finally struck that allowed Murphy to play for Great Britain on the Saturday provided he turned out for the RAF against Leicester Tigers two days earlier. Compromise arrangements like these continued until he was released by the RAF in autumn 1962.

By far the majority of the leaguers who made an impression were threequarters. For those making up the rest of the team there were major problems adjusting as the two games were clearly continuing to diverge, especially in the areas of forward and half-back play. Alex Murphy, as mentioned above a world class half-back for his native St Helens RLFC, was more appropriately played at stand-off in the RAF XV where his pace and ability to create breaks could be better utilised. Almost all the Servicemen attached to rugby league clubs who were selected to pack down in an Inter-Services match were converts from senior rugby union. The one real exception being Jack Scroby, a loose-forward for Bradford Northern (and later Halifax) who won a place in the Army pack, but even he had played rugby union for his grammar school in Halifax.

Fortunately the external threat to Britain was never sufficiently strong for rugby league to be granted the same rights during the era of National Service as it had enjoyed during the Second World War. Consequently, there were no grand initiatives of the kind that the Army's Northern Command had promoted during wartime with the result that the two games progressed little further during the era of National Service than they had in peacetime – individual talents such as Ike Southward and Alex Murphy were recognised by many within rugby union and fraternisation was tacitly understood to be beneficial rather than harmful, but sadly nothing more. With the attitudes prevailing in civilian rugby union at the time, the sporting camaraderie built up during those short Service interludes proved insufficient to bring any significant change.

A changing perception of the external threat and a growing unpopularity at home after the Suez debacle led to National Service being scaled down from the late 1950s onwards. Numbers fell as deferments increased until finally the call-up was ended at the start of 1961, what remained of that last intake being demobbed in May 1963. With its passing the Armed Forces returned to being the home of the regular serviceman. Its passing also brought to an end the most extensive period of officially condoned interaction between the two games.

For love or money?

The end of the high profile, almost formal co-operation of the National Service era gave way to a time of more individual contact. Where both games were active it was almost impossible for contact not to occur. While it was possible within the rugby league heartlands to grow up playing that game and no other, there was no exclusivity. Outside the North the situation was very different and contacts had to be handled with great tact. Having already 'gone north', a spell in the RAF changed the mind of one young Welshman regarding his future and caused a restatement of the RFU's laws on professionalism.

Aged just seventeen and still at secondary school, Glyn John had left Bridgend RUFC for Leigh RLFC in September 1949, collecting a signing-on fee of £400 in the process. After making three appearances on the wing just before the turn of the year, John changed his mind about the course he had taken. He applied for reinstatement as an amateur, his father repaying the signing-on fee to Leigh. One of the arguments that helped convince the Welsh RU to grant reinstatement was that John had legally been a minor when he had signed a rugby league contract. John's reinstatement led to the rules on professionalism being amended. The age under which a school leaver could not be considered a professional by signing a rugby league form or through any other connection was raised from 17 to 18, even though RFL rules allowed a player to sign as a professional upon his 16th birthday.

That amendment formalised what had been an accepted practice in some northern districts for many years. Balancing the demands of locality and future educational advancement was a problem for many boys, especially when family ties were strong. Bev Risman, the son of the great Gus, was educated at Cockermouth Grammar School where he gained selection for England Schools rugby union under-18 teams in 1956 and 1957. He has recounted how after playing union for his school on Saturday, he would switch to league on Sunday. After his 18th birthday it had to be union exclusively as he went on to Manchester University and later Loughborough Colleges, gaining selection for England and the British Lions along the way. While he was one of the most famous, he was by no means the only young man to enjoy playing both games.

It was understood that the opportunity to progress on to college or university meant some involvement with rugby union. In the north of

England it created a situation in which a league upbringing could still have some influence on the union game, particularly if the boy stayed on at school. There was no hiding it and in some districts the league influence was so strong it could be detected in the way the first teams of the leading schools played the game. If a team prized possession and refused to kick it away, and relished every opportunity to engage in movements based on passing and running that combined the forwards and the backs then it clearly had a league core. Any debts to the league game were, of course, strenuously denied.

At that age the natural rugby skills of running and handling had yet not been overridden in the union game by physical size and the complexities of set-piece technique. So it was possible for a team built around a league core to be very successful in schools union even against opponents from dyed in 'the wool union districts. That kind of team certainly had thrived in St Helens before, but reached new heights when Ray French, having risen through the town's rugby union club to the England team, returned after university to join the staff at his old school, Cowley. Although by now a professional with the town's rugby league club, French concentrated on raising the standard of the school's rugby union team. During his time at Cowley he turned the school into one of the most successful and productive rugby union nurseries in the north of England. Out through Cowley's gates there flowed a rich stream of talented players many of whom went on to reach the highest level in both rugby codes.

For some of those leaving Cowley their schooldays had fired a desire to reach the top at rugby union, while for others union was at best an adjunct to their career, or perhaps for the majority it was no more than an enjoyable social game that might rekindle their enthusiasm and desire to play top class sport once more. Some of them would choose to remain in union. What was galling for the union game was that invariably a significant proportion of those youngsters would return to league, to a game they knew, had enjoyed previously and which to them was synonymous with top class rugby in their area.

Bringing a union player with some league background back into the professional game was a far less risky business than taking a chance on a complete union novice. Not surprisingly, many were approached and if interested would often be asked to have a trial. One of the thousands of young men to take part in a trial was Ian Ball, a star pupil from Ray French's Cowley nursery, who had been making a name for himself in rugby union. Following in his father, Joe's, footsteps Ball headed to Barrow where he turned out for the home side against Leeds in autumn 1978 under the pseudonym A. N. Other. Such a pseudonym or the equally popular S. O. Else or A. Newman were regularly to be found in league programmes. All this subterfuge was necessary to try and obscure Ball's true identity, which was in theory known only to the RFL, the club coach and some members of the board. Mostly this minimal cover was adequate because all associated with the game of rugby played their part, whether they were his union teammates, club officials or watching journalists. Only if Ball signed, which he did the following day, would the latter deem to publish his name. If the trial went badly or he declined the offer Ball could still have returned to his union career with Wasps. If not and his name was made public he would have to be banned for life. As league did not want that to happen because it would deter future trialists and union did not want it either as it would force too many players out of the game the whole contrived practice carried on for years.

The easiest way for league's detractors to explain this desire to return to league was to write it off as being purely driven by financial gain. How else could someone decide to turn their backs on union, a game played for love to return to a game they... loved more? That surely could not be. This negative image was reinforced by those in rugby league who saw any youngster who decided to have a spell playing union as doing it solely to push up his signing-on fee when he eventually returned to league.

Love for the league game did not always carry the day. At all levels league, whether amateur or professional, was driven by an overwhelming competitive spirit and it was not just some youngsters who wanted a less demanding alternative. So too did many veterans, who, given some encouragement, would sign up with a nearby junior union club to play in its lower social XVs. It was a non-harmful arrangement and generally went well until the league elements were 'discovered' and rooted out.

All this subterfuge and hypocrisy resulted directly from the RFU not being prepared to treat the issue of professionalism as a perfectly legal commercial matter, preferring instead to see it as a moral issue. By dealing with it on a contractual footing, it would have been possible for everyone to be treated as having the best interests of the rugby game at heart, even if they were operating in rather different playing environments.

Unity and strength

Association football had faced up to the issue of professionalism in the 1880s and accepted it not without difficulty. What threats that code had faced to its unity had been localised and even when as a result of some serious difficulties in the south of England a split in the FA had occurred, it had been short-lived. Even the Scots who had seen large numbers of players migrate to England had learnt to live with professionalism. Despite occasional media speculation about the possibilities it might offer, there were hardly any serious attempts to bring the two rugby games back together. The first semi-official possibility was brought to public attention was 20 years after the original 'split' when association football – the game to gain most – was at its most aggressive in moving into northern rugby areas.

Bruised from the loss of Stockport and the surrender of half of Bradford, the NRL was bracing itself for further bad news in 1905-06 when Hull City and Leeds City made their debuts in the Second Division of the Football League. Having been forced to end their tenancy at the Boulevard by a Northern Union ruling prohibiting the sharing of grounds with Football League clubs, Hull City outbid Hull and East Riding RUFC to take over the tenancy at Hull Cricket Club's Circle ground. At short notice Hull and East Riding were forced to take refuge at City's old, undeveloped Dairycoates ground.

This situation seems to have focused the minds of many of Hull's leading rugby supporters. Believing that a new consensus was emerging Hull FC took the initiative through a letter to the NU committee meeting in October 1905. Hull's proposal called for discussions to be opened with the RFU with the aim of creating a new body similar to the FA that would represent both amateur and professional interests. Support for this initiative came from Barrow, a town feeling the impact of Barrow AFC reaching the First Division of the Lancashire Combination. Many Northern Union supporters were horrified by this proposal, seeing it as naïve and giving the impression that the Northern Union had lost its nerve. By the time it came to the following month's NU committee, the proposal received no support and was allowed to fall.

There was undoubtedly widespread sympathy for moves towards unity in the North. Twelve months later at the dinner following Yorkshire RU's match against the Springboks at Headingley the speeches returned to the issue of the continuing split in rugby. Arthur Hartley, the representative of the Yorkshire RU on the RFU committee in making the speech of thanks to the host club took a positive stance – reminding his audience that the Leeds Cricket, Football and Athletic Club (CF&AC) had made its gesture of goodwill despite its differences with the Yorkshire RU and had in so doing set an example that the RFU might well follow. Next to speak was the president of Leeds NUFC, Joshua Sheldon, and he tried to bring a touch of economic reality to the proceedings by drawing upon his own experiences of the devastating effect association football had had on the game of rugby within the city of Leeds. Leeds United's first season in the Football League, 1905-06, had halved the average attendance at Headingley and caused them to incur a loss despite a reasonably good playing record in the NRL. While he hoped for a healing of the split as being in the best interests of the game as a whole, Sheldon was aware of the need for a senior club to make the investment in their operations pay. He therefore made the point that to move forward together the Headingley grounds like many others needed "... something more than the game as played by rugby union clubs" could provide. Sheldon's point, which probably meant the acceptance of the NRL by the RFU, fell on stony ground.

The pressure of professional soccer was insistent and within a couple of months it looked as though Bradford as a whole would sever all its' professional links to the rugby game. Even though they had won the Yorkshire Cup at the start of December 1906, the management of Bradford were unhappy with their inability to attract enough spectators through the gates to pay their way and as large losses loomed they began to look for an alternative winter game. Initially it looked as though a return to rugby union was the management's favoured option. In furtherance of that aim a meeting with the RFU committee was arranged after the Calcutta Cup match at Blackheath on Saturday 16 March 1907. Having heard of the club's plight, the RFU subsequently announced that rather than let it die they would allow re-admittance on strictly amateur terms. Believing this was an attractive offer, the RFU asked that Bradford's main officers make it public in case any other NRL members would want to take advantage.

At a meeting in mid-April the membership of the rugby club voted to accept the RFU's offer. Having abandoned the Northern Union the club awaited details of the prestige fixtures that the RFU had guaranteed to replace the NRL programme. In readiness for its return to the RFU, the club prepared to release all its professional players and any paid officers at the end of the season. Meanwhile those that really mattered, the main financial backers of the overall Park Avenue complex, were not convinced. After taking legal advice, the rugby club's decision was ruled invalid and a new association football club established to replace the rugby club with the express intention of gaining a place in the Football League. It was a traumatic loss for both rugby games, not only of a senior club, but also of Park Avenue, one of the best appointed grounds in the North. The responsibility for rebuilding a senior rugby team and securing a new ground fell on the shoulders of the local Northern Union supporters. To make sure there was no misunderstanding, the new club added the suffix Northern in September 1907 so that everyone knew at a glance what kind of rugby it would be playing. Despite major difficulties, Bradford Northern set out to continue the city's long tradition in the handling game. If losses on this scale could not dent the RFU's faith in absolute amateurism then the best that could be achieved was for the two games to continue to be played in parallel.

Where association football's incursion had failed, some of rugby's leading figures believed four years of acute national trauma might succeed. Just over two weeks after the signing of the Armistice a Yorkshire RU XV met a Northern Command Military team, containing a number of Northern Union men at Headingley in aid of military charities. At the post match dinner the speakers brought out into the open all the peacetime problems that were bound to beset relations between the RFU and the Northern Union. Barron Kilner of Wakefield RUFC, after stating his own opposition to professionalism, hoped that the heads of the two unions could devise a scheme to enable players to play together in peace and as in wartime. He was supported in this by Sir W. A. Forster Todd, the Lord Mayor of York. Continuing in this vein, J. B. Cooke of Wakefield Trinity expressed his opinion that all present were in spirit rugby men. If nothing else he hoped that charity matches could continue in peacetime. After all, if they could not unite in the interests of the game, they might at least do so in the cause of humanity. However, two other speakers J. A. Miller and the old English rugby union international, J. L. Hickson, took a different stance. Neither of those Yorkshire RU stalwarts saw any possibility of the RFU relaxing its principled opposition to professionalism and the best they could foresee was that those who had served in the First World War would be reinstated. As Hickson saw it, men who were fit to fight for their King and country were good enough to be made amateurs in rugby football if they so desired. In reality, however, he felt that even the acceptance of reinstatement for former comrades in arms, let alone munitions workers, was unlikely to gain favour with the majority of the RFU. And if it had it would undoubtedly have fallen foul of the Irish and Scottish unions at the IRB. Professionalism had once more put an end to any prospect of progress.

If neither the loss of large swathes of the northern rugby heartlands to a competitor game nor even the loss of the flower of the nation's youth in the First World War could change the RFU's stance then it was unlikely that there was any prospect of future approaches being successful. Occasionally journalists would resurrect the idea, but in practice there appeared to be no chance of reunification while pristine amateurism dominated the mindset of the RFU, and that proved to be the case. In its absence, the RFL was left to assume responsibility for resisting the incursions of the Football League and in keeping alive the local rugby traditions of the northern counties. For this it would receive no credit. Belatedly the RFU would show its appreciation for the League's efforts over the years when it sought to exploit those reserves of rugby talent and support for its own ends.

Whose rules?

By then, even if professionalism could have been taken out of the equation, there would still have remained the issue of the differences in playing laws to be resolved. Although the Northern Union had started life using the laws of the RFU, most of its leaders understood that those laws made it extremely difficult to play entertaining football and secure victory at the same time. To sustain professionalism, which was legalised by the Northern Union in July 1898, the game had to provide entertainment for the paying spectator otherwise it would not survive.

To try and improve the situation, the Northern Union began to make changes that would reduce roughness and interference, and help the game succeed as a spectator friendly sport. To help it in the latter case, the scoring values were standardised at three points for a try and two for all goals in July 1897. At the same AGM the view took hold that it was impossible to reform the line-out and make it less likely to end in a scrum. Initially the line-out was replaced by a punt-out, but when it too was found to lead to scrappy and often rough play it was succeeded by a scrum in 1902. To reduce the number of stoppages the knock-on law was liberalised to allow a 'cricket catch' in July 1901. Yet in total these changes proved insufficient to meet the challenge that association football was presenting.

Out of necessity, the Northern Union passed a series of amendments in June 1906 that marked a decisive break with the laws of the RFU. Taken as a whole, the three changes met the need to keep the ball on the field, in play and as visible as possible for the spectators. Firstly, kicking to touch would only gain ground if the ball bounced before going into touch – if it did not play would restart from where the ball was kicked. Secondly, to reduce injury and return the ball into play without the need for a scrum the tackled player was required to first regain his feet before dropping the ball after which it could be played by either side. Finally, to provide more space for open play and so reduce the amount of mauling that was thought to be blighting matches the number of players in a team was reduced to 13, which although not stipulated meant in practice the removal of two forwards.

It had taken 10 years, but the legislators had finally got the balance right. Four less players on the field provided extra space for the backs to exploit. The new touch law curbed the aimless punting to touch that had often previously blighted matches. Altogether it meant the spectators could more easily follow the play – something that was considered to be a key factor in association football's growing popularity. There was considerable sympathy for the Northern Union's new laws within English rugby, particularly from those districts like Coventry and south Devon that were soon to come under severe threat from the expansion of association football's Southern League. Unfortunately any expressions of support from within the RFU led to expulsion rather than discussion.

Although the key elements of rugby league football had been put in place one of them, the play-the-ball would require constant attention. The play-the-ball's prime function was to restart play after the tackle, but was too often blighted by interference and barging. It took 20 years before the modern form of the play-the-ball was finally put in place. Acting upon proposals from the New South Wales RFL, the loose scrummage that still formed around the tackled player was abolished in the summer of 1927. In future only the tackled player, the tackler and two acting half-backs would be allowed to take part in the play-the-ball.

By creating its own separate set of laws the Northern Union and later the RFL was attempting, not without difficulty, to create a game equally friendly to both players and spectators. Consideration of the latter's interests was an anathema to the RFU for many years and for them to have played a part in the process rendered all the Northern Union's and subsequently all rugby league's changes professionally inspired. It was not until the late 1960s that the RFU showed signs of dropping this attitude.

While it appears that the movement was always away from the laws of rugby union, there was a time in the life of Rugby League when it seemed possible that it would begin to flow in the opposite direction. As so often in the history of the game the focus for that possibility was the return of the ball into play after it had gone into touch and the need to improve the restart after the tackle.

Although he attended the soccer-playing Barrow Grammar School, Bill Fallowfield, the son and nephew of two former players with Barrow NUFC, found time outside its gates to play rugby league well enough to win a place in the Barrow and District under-18 team. After leaving the Grammar School for Cambridge University in the early 1930s Bill Fallowfield integrated himself fully into rugby union. Although he did not win a Blue, Fallowfield went on to gain recognition for his wing-forward play with Northampton and the East Midlands before seeing war service with the RAF, during which he appeared in two Service internationals. His breadth of rugby experience and youthful enthusiasm seemed to mark out Flight Lieutenant Fallowfield as ideal secretary material when he submitted his application to the RFL. The RL Council agreed and Fallowfield took over as general secretary of the RFL on 1 January 1946.

Initially Fallowfield focused on the scrum which was required to return the ball back into play after it had gone into touch. His preference was to replace the scrum with a throw-in and a number of trial matches were held to see how it would work in practice. Many thought the throw-in was an improvement, although concerns were expressed about it making the game too fast. Having taken it that far, Fallowfield seems to have allowed the momentum to dissipate and he moved on to the question of the play-the-ball, which most commentators agreed was far more pressing.

Since the end of the Second World War the practice at the play-the-ball had deteriorated to the extent that it bore little resemblance to a meaningful contest for the ball. Unless he made a mistake, the player tackled in possession was almost certain to heel the ball back to his own side. What had once been seen as the means to create open play was now seen to be stifling it. Various changes to the play-the-ball were tried with little success when Fallowfield came up with a very radical alternative.

Legend has it that Fallowfield embarked on to this course following comments about the stop-and-start nature of the play-the-ball made by the Duke of Edinburgh while a guest of honour at the Cup Final. Whatever the reason, something spurred the RL Council into action for in June 1955 it ruled that all the pre-season friendlies scheduled for mid-August would use the rugby union tackle law instead of the play-the-ball. Not all the members agreed and Castleford and Wakefield Trinity cancelled their fixture rather than go through the upheaval of adapting to the new trial law. All the others went ahead, but in general the crowds were none too impressed and the 'improvement' was widely condemned.

With most of the clubs far from convinced, Fallowfield realised he would have to keep campaigning if a law change was to be brought about. To try and achieve that, an exhibition match between Leigh and Oldham was held at Odsal in October 1956 to check public reaction. Although both teams had a sprinkling of rugby union experience, lack of familiarity undervalued the match and the players expressed their opinion that this was the wrong course to follow to the game's administrators. Five years later, Fallowfield made one last push. Once again, this time in conjunction with the French League, an exhibition match was staged at the Parc des Princes in Paris in October 1961.There two invitation teams containing a large number of players with top flight union experience tried to make the experimental law work. Unfortunately the change was blamed for producing too many scrums, too much speculative kicking and chaotic loose scrums.

The possibility of introducing the rugby union release was effectively ended by that match, although Fallowfield defiantly proclaimed that in his opinion the rugby union release remained the simplest and best option. Other options began to be considered and five years later the RFL settled on the limited tackle law as its formula for open play. That very radical alternative took the league game a long way from its origins and saw it accused of abandoning all the classic elements of the union game. As with all aspects of the split in rugby, the differences meant a huge amount to those inside its world, but mostly very little to those outside.

One game?

Generally, once a law change had been made by one game, it immediately became taboo for the other. Needing something different to counter the growing influence of league, the Australian and New Zealand Unions convinced the IRB in March 1968 to make a change that rewarded positive play. Breaking with past practice, the change, adopted on an experimental basis, mimicked the rugby league law and prevented territorial gains being made from kicks made beyond the 25-yard line that went into touch on the full. Twelve months later the change was declared a great success and written permanently into the laws. Its impact was to bring a new dimension to back play just as it had to rugby league 60 years earlier. Deciding that other changes might be advantageous, the IRB meeting in March 1972 agreed to amend the knock-on to allow a 'cricket catch' once more on a 12 month experimental basis. In line with league's experience this change also proved to be a resounding success and was made permanent.

Around the same time, the RFU, responding to pressure from the membership, began to adopt a critical part of rugby league's legacy of trophies and big occasions by allowing a national knockout cup and a rudimentary league competition to be launched. Even coaching and coaches were welcomed into the fold and found to be not only respectable, but indispensable. Professionalism however still remained an anathema.

As well as adopting elements of the rugby league's rules and competitive formats, the RFU increasingly began to take the opportunity of a common ancestry to represent the entire rugby game, especially on state bodies such as the Sports Council and this obviously led to friction. To try and make sure that valuable sources of funding were not lost, many rugby league activists found themselves having to defend their game's independence. Rather than squabble over that common ancestry, many within rugby league's ranks began to celebrate their game's differences and its qualities. No longer was league just the professional variant of rugby union; it was a significantly, if not entirely different game.

It could not be denied that after nearly 80 years the respective playing styles were very far apart – so far apart that many players could not cross the divide between them. For nearly all that time most commentators had presented rugby union as **the** rugby game, with league very much in its shadow. It was the failure of some of its leading media figures to counter this by presenting the game in a way that could make its strategy and tactics more understandable that particularly angered and frustrated most of league's supporters.

There was a marked improvement in that situation when Ray French was appointed as the BBC's rugby league commentator in 1981. A couple of years earlier, French had published his autobiography in which he had advanced the view that the games' common ancestry still mattered. In fact, in his opinion, union had devalued some of the common skills it shared with league – namely handling and running – and needed to recover them. This view, which he reiterated in future books and incorporated in his work as a schoolboy coach, was well received in the early 1980s.

French found vital allies in the shape of a group of Australian rugby league players. Few, if any, touring teams to this country have ever had a greater impact on their destination than the 1982 Kangaroos. Their performances across the north of England left the crowds gasping in awe. Suddenly the possibilities of modern rugby league were being unfolded in front of their eyes and it was much appreciated. Thanks to those Australians, rugby league rediscovered its voice. Suddenly after nearly half a century of quiescence, Britain's rugby league coaches woke up and began to produce manuals extolling the skills and strategies needed to play their game successfully. Word quickly spread and soon amongst the crowds there could be found union coaches and supporters, keen to look and learn from modern rugby league.

Despite some significant reservations about the game, Carwyn James retained his respect for rugby league and was clearly impressed by the visit of the Kangaroos. Following their tour he wrote in *The Guardian* that "The Australians left no one in Britain in doubt as to their athleticism, superb fitness, teamwork and flawless handling. Whereas the curse of the union game is nine- or 10-man rugby, the curse of the league is the blinkered, bulldozing tactic of one-man rugby. The Australians, however, have clearly restored the art of collision rugby allied to support play which leads to thrilling, sustained movements."

Sadly James' untimely death in January 1983 robbed the rugby world of a chance to see how he would have incorporated the lessons he drew from the Australians' visit into the play of the British rugby unions.

Their departure left English rugby in a state of shock – league wondering how it could match the Australians' standards, union trying to comprehend how a game it had publicly written off could produce such exciting football. Suddenly rugby league was being publicly appreciated to an unparalleled extent by leading figures in the northern rugby union world. Bill Beaumont extolled the Kangaroos' virtues and described himself as a fair weather Wigan supporter. Steve Smith went even further and stated that "Australian rugby league ... is the finest ball sport I have ever seen". Dick Greenwood the former England coach thought that videos of the tests should be mandatory viewing for all prospective England rugby union internationals. Praise indeed and richly deserved. While English league struggled to elevate its domestic game to the Australians' level, it found itself thrust into an unaccustomed leadership position in terms of rugby's development.

Had he lived, Carwyn James' status within British rugby union might have made it possible for him to openly incorporate ideas from the Wallabies and by implication the Kangaroos. He had, according to his biographer Alun Richards, already discreetly crossed the line in his preparations for the 1971 Lions tour. Seeking ideas, he had made contact with Dave Sexton then manger at Manchester United to review that club's training schedules. His second appointment had taken him a little further north, to Wigan RFLC where he met with their coach, Eric Ashton, to study his techniques. It is interesting to speculate whether even he would have faced the sort of protests that greeted the news that a group of leading rugby union coaches had been on a fact finding mission to the north of England. At the start of November 1985 Bath RUFC's coaching team – the head coach, Jack Rowell, and his two assistants, coach, Dave Robson, and the conditioner, Tom Hudson, – shocked some of the RFU hierarchy by spending a few days with Hull K.R., the holders of the Rugby

League Championship and the Regal Trophy. In their striving to make Bath the best, the trio wanted to study the methods of Roger Millward, the Rovers' coach. Their visit proved controversial and drew a sharp reprimand from the RFU. It certainly did the trio no harm as Bath went on to complete a decade of success that ranked it as the most outstanding club side in rugby union history. However, it did mean that other rugby union coaches were far more circumspect about announcing their appreciation or even attendance at future Kangaroo fixtures.

Four years later, while the 'Invincibles' still lived in the English sporting memory, another Kangaroo party arrived and had an almost equal impact. Once more the Kangaroos proved masters of the game and led many more to substantially change their perception of league. One who publicly expressed his admiration for the Kangaroos and their style of play was Clem Thomas, the former Welsh rugby union international flanker and journalist. Having taken a week to reflect on another test series drubbing for Great Britain in 1986, Thomas wrote in *The Observer* on Sunday 30 November that for him "After nearly 40 years in the opposition camp, I now believe rugby league is a better game to watch and play than rugby union. In stating my heresy, I have met surprisingly few arguments from my union friends, indeed the majority agree with me."

Conclusions such as this were seized avidly by supporters of rugby league as a sign that the true merits of their game were being recognised at last. For a game with a significant inferiority complex born out of years of isolation, such glowing compliments were made all the sweeter for the fact that they came in the main from people outside the north of England. Professionalism was at last being recognised as a mental attitude, a state of preparation, not just a question of remuneration.

To the 'Invincibles' and their successors the 'Unbeatables', as the 1982 and 1986 teams were nicknamed respectively, rugby league owes a huge debt for between them changing the game's perception in the eyes of England's sporting public. Attitudes often frozen for decades began to change especially within the coaching fraternity and caused the game, ostracised for so long to be reassessed. In chasing the same levels of excitement and the same levels of performance, rugby union's hard working coaches were steering a course that was leading their game perilously towards the same powerful currents that had ripped it apart ninety years earlier. Not surprisingly the futures of the two games appeared once again destined to become more closely intertwined.

Rugby league: Give it a try

It had taken 90 years, but as the 'Unbeatables' departed Britain's shores there were at last signs that rugby league would finally get the respect it deserved. The respect lavished on the Kangaroos had changed the atmosphere between the two games. Thanks to those Australians, a game

1980s Australian rugby league star Brett Kenny.
(Photo: David Williams)

1980s Great Britain rugby league winger Des Drummond.
(Photo: David Williams)

that had been depicted as being so tainted by professionalism that its rules could not even be sampled by an amateur without almost certain corruption was seen to have merit. Suddenly this extreme stance, which had been justified on the grounds that it was the only way to keep the union world pure, was clearly discredited.

At long last the idea that most amateur rugby league players were the devil incarnate was swept away and they were granted the same opportunity as all other amateur sportsmen to be able to play rugby union where and when they chose. The 'free gangway' as it was dubbed was finally opened by the IRB at its meeting in late March 1987. Making something legal can only get rid of the stigma; it cannot automatically overcome the prejudices, suspicions and misconceptions built up over so many generations. There was to be no immediate mass migration between the two games; club loyalty being far too strong for such an overnight change to occur.

Slowly but surely, signs emerged that rugby's amateurs were keen to make contact and even cooperate where it made sense. Within weeks of being opened, the free gangway was proving useful, at least when it came to the use of facilities. As a result of Blackpool Borough pulling out of the town, the Blackpool Rugby League Supporters' Club was left without a venue for its annual seven-a-side tournament. Their problems were solved by an offer to use the facilities of Fleetwood RUFC, an act that would have meant expulsion only weeks earlier. It was not just in the rugby league heartlands that such assistance could be found. Wasps RUFC stepped forward in 1988 and offered their old Sudbury home as a possible long-term home for the London Amateur Rugby League's Cup Final day. And in the north-east, Hartlepool ARLFC managed to secure agreement to share facilities with a local union club.

Using each other's facilities was practical, but the possibilities now opened up led once more to far more fanciful ideas. Ninety years on, there remained a fascination with what English rugby had lost and what combined potential it might unleash in the future if it could overcome its disunity. To try and ascertain what might be possible, there was a pressing need to find out just how much of a common heritage still existed. One of the earliest, if not the first, place in England where that curiosity moved on to something more practical was the city of Kingston-upon-Hull. For the final match at The Circle before moving to a new ground, the members of Hull and East Riding, the region's premier rugby union club for nearly 90 years chose a most radical option. They decided to invite their near neighbours West Hull ARLFC, the reigning national amateur rugby league champions. The match which took place on Sunday 21 May 1989 was played with one half under league and one half under union rules. In the best traditions of such cross-code encounters all the proceeds were donated to charity.

This and other future initiatives to cross the great divide came as the two games were in the process of moving even further apart on the field, largely as a result of league replacing the scrum on the sixth tackle with a handover. Suddenly scrums were so low in number that they were almost irrelevant. In 1989 Ray French published *More Kinds of Rugby,* which included a discussion of the problems facing a player converting from union to league. French drew on the experience of David Stephenson, a centre threequarter, who had successfully made the transition nearly 10 years earlier. Stephenson, who had recently made his 10th test appearance for Great Britain to compliment his eight appearances for the English rugby union schools under-19 team, had this to say: "It is harder than ever for a player to switch codes because the two games have changed so much. In the forwards I can only see a union flank forward having the pace, tackling ability and footballing skills to make the change successfully. In the backs it is much easier but I can see few union players in Britain having the running opportunities to impress their skills on a league scout."

Now that the opportunity was finally presenting itself, at least for the amateurs, the chance for the two games to learn something from each other at top level seemed more remote than ever. As the common thread weakened there appeared to be less and less likelihood that meaningful contact would be maintained. Without any initiative on the horizon to rescue the situation, it looked likely that the two games were destined to become further estranged.

Out in the open

Six years later the IRB's unexpected decision to throw the game open led to a totally new situation as commercial interests were able to get more involved in the day to day running of the game. At first the RFU tried to put off the task of reinventing itself as an openly commercial game for 12 months, but the tide of change could not be held back and soon there were the first signs of a thaw in relations at professional level. Many were caught by surprise when that thaw soon appeared to be heading for total meltdown. Anyone not aware of the history could have easily thought that the two games had had to be forcibly and artificially kept apart for the past century as they eagerly sought ways to make up and be friends.

Some saw the IRB's decision as opening the way to a rapid reunification of the two games. David Adams, a rugby league coach, referee and director of Halifax RLFC, rushed in to print and published, in October 1995 a complete and detailed set of *United Rugby Rules.* It was undoubtedly a premature move as the necessary rational debate was never a realistic possibility. Far too many vested interests were tied into the rival games for such a process to occur.

49

What those commercial interests did ensure was that the old one-way street, which for a century had headed due north suddenly appeared to have reversed direction. A number of leading players who had previously switched from rugby union grabbed the opportunity when it presented itself to return to their roots, taking their acquired league influences with them. The most prominent to make the move was Jonathan Davies whose transfer from Warrington cost Cardiff RUFC a fee of £100,000 and a sizable contract at the end of October. Coaches with a league background were also being lined up to assist their union counterparts.

After an interval of nearly 50 years, the prohibition on stadium usage was rapidly dropped. There was no more startling demonstration of the new reality than the announcement by the London Broncos that they would be playing four matches at The Stoop, the home of Harlequins RUFC, during November. Less glamorous, but equally important, was a similar invitation that same month for Carlisle to play three 'home' matches at Carlisle RUFC, a club that had been implacably opposed to the rugby league game for a century. By early January, the soon-to-be homeless Leeds RUFC were able to announce an agreement with Leeds CF&AC, the owners of Leeds RLFC to play at Headingley for the following five seasons. As commentators struggled to predict where it would all end the biggest unanswered question remained, could the two games get together on the field after so long.

As rugby league's controversially truncated Centenary season drew to a close in mid-January 1996 the biggest club name in English rugby league, Wigan, was considering ways to pay the bills until the first summer season could begin. The neighbouring senior rugby union club, Orrell, was invited to play their two biggest Courage league fixtures at Central Park, against Leicester and Bath, both lost on 30 March and 20 April respectively. As an exercise in checking crowd potential it was a failure as the local league fans shunned the matches and the attendance failed to pass two thousand on either occasion. When viewed in conjunction with other negotiations that were just breaking into the public domain, those matches convinced many league fans that some form of reunification was being actively pursued. Much suspicion focused on Maurice Lindsay, the chief executive of the RFL and formerly the chairman of Wigan RLFC, and the possibility that he was using his position to prepare the ground for a Murdoch-inspired merger of the two games.

Lindsay did nothing to allay those suspicions by appearing more than happy to go along with a proposition put forward by Alan McColm, a leading player agent. McColm had earlier approached Wigan and the biggest club in English rugby union, Bath with ideas for a groundbreaking cross-code encounter, Rugby Challenge 96. For purely financial reasons both clubs were interested – Wigan, having been denied a Wembley pay day for the first time in nine years were struggling to meet their existing wage bill, Bath to fund the new contract payments that were soon to fall

From league to union

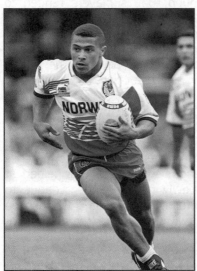

Top: Henry Paul – on the left playing league for Bradford Bulls, on the right playing union for Gloucester.
Bottom: Jason Robinson, on the left playing league for Wigan, on the right playing union for Sale.
Both players played for Wigan against Bath in the 1996 cross-code challenge.
(Photos: David Williams)

due. McColm's proposal was for the clubs to meet twice – once under league and once under union rules. To host the expected crowds, McColm proposed that two neutral grounds be used. Save and Prosper agreed to sponsor the matches and after some initial resistance the RFU sanctioned the project. Bath's playing staff, although in turmoil as they considered various contract offers, were still amateur and during February one of the most prominent, Jeremy Guscott, refused to be involved in either of the matches, claiming they were "a pointless exercise". His coach, John Hall, was far more enthusiastic and on the eve of the first match called openly for a merger of the two games.

The first of those two historic matches took place, under rugby league rules at Manchester City FC's old ground, Maine Road, on the evening of Wednesday 8 May 1996 – just four days after Bath had beaten Leicester in the Pilkington Cup Final and two days after English rugby union was formally declared open. By way of preparation, Bath met a South Wales amateur XIII and suffered a defeat by eight tries to four! Even with some assistance from the former Welsh rugby union international and current coach to the Wales rugby league team, Clive Griffiths, Bath were desperately short of effective preparation and were soon floundering. Unable to shake off their union background, Bath's players tended to follow the ball thereby weakening their organisation particularly on defence. Wigan's players, playing their own game, enjoyed themselves running in 16 tries in the 82-6 rout in front of a crowd of 20,418. Despite the one-sidedness of the match, the strength and pace of the Wigan team, its lines of running, general handling and use of space were widely complimented.

Between the two legs of the cross-code challenge there was further evidence of a new relationship between the two games. Wigan had been offered and accepted a special invite to take part in the Middlesex RU Sevens Tournament long before the dates of the two challenge matches had been finalised. To ensure a full strength squad could be fielded at Twickenham, Wigan arranged with the newly formed Super League to postpone their weekend fixture until the following Tuesday. It looked a foolhardy decision especially when Bath withdrew from the Sevens at short notice. It was a historic moment for Wigan and the game as a whole when on Saturday 11 May 1996 their seven became the first rugby league team ever to set foot on Twickenham's turf. The realisation slowly spread over the 61,000 crowd that they might be watching something truly amazing as Wigan accounted for Richmond, then Harlequins and finally Leicester to reach the Final. Briefly it appeared likely that Wasps would deny Wigan the trophy as their seven quickly moved into a 15-0 lead. Throughout the tournament the Wigan seven had given the impression that if they could get the ball they could score almost at will and when it mattered they proved their point. Wasps were left reeling as Wigan proceeded to run in six tries without reply, to gain an easy victory by 38-15. Besides the Russell Cargill trophy, Wigan also received a cheque for £20,000 for donation to their nominated charity – the Wigan Schools Rugby League Association. For the first time ever, a Twickenham crowd had had the chance to cheer a supreme performance by a league team whose pace and support play had proved to many of them a revelation.

Having taken the opportunity of some training sessions with Orrell Wigan returned to Twickenham for the second-leg of the Challenge on Saturday 25 May in a cautiously optimistic mood. By fielding some players with previous senior rugby union experience such as Scott Quinnell, Martin Offiah and the former All Black, Inga Tuigamala, Wigan were hoping to put up a stern challenge. In addition there were three players with youthful union experience, current stand-off, Shaun Edwards, who had once captained the England Schools rugby union under-16 team and two others who had been enjoying their retirement, namely former centre, Joe Lydon, (aged 32, but once an England Schools rugby union under-18 cap) and second-row forward, Graeme West, (aged 42). Realistically, even though the latter pair regularly turned out for Wigan RUFC's veterans' team, they really had no chance of living with the pace. After the shock of the first encounter, this match demonstrated clearly how far the two games and their players had diverged. Exploiting their own rules, Bath ensured that Wigan's challenge would be short-lived by keeping the game among the forwards where their tighter scrummaging could be brought to bear. With very few scrums in a rugby league match and nearly all of them un-contested, Wigan's front-row were unprepared to handle Bath's drive in the set pieces. Fortunately for Wigan's props, their Bath counterparts, not wishing to cause injury, were very restrained. So for the best part of the first hour Bath kept it tight and made sure that Wigan would be denied sufficient possession to exhibit their attacking flair to the 50,000 crowd. Leading 39-0 after 50 minutes, Bath relaxed their forward grip a little and opened out play whereupon Wigan promptly exploited the space made available to run in three flamboyant tries to finish 44-19 down.

Thanks to that late flourish, Wigan made sure of finishing as winners on points aggregate and both clubs got what they most wanted in the short-term, nearly a quarter of a million pounds each to help meet their need for cash. At the post-match press conference the chief executives of the RFL and the RFU, Maurice Lindsay and Tony Hallet respectively, were extremely positive and enthusiastic about the Challenge and the prospects it had opened up for the future. Having tried to curb the enthusiasm for such events a few months earlier, Lindsay now found himself expressing the wildly optimistic opinion that there would be a single game in five years time.

What next?

Reunification was a much bigger challenge than Lindsay possibly realised at the time. Still there was much to celebrate. For one thing the unthinkable had happened; rugby union had accepted professionalism and the world had not ended. On the up-side, the cross-code challenges had had a very positive effect in helping to overcome some of the historic bitterness that had characterised relations between league and union. It also served to highlight just how much deep seated hostility remained. On the down-side, those matches had also shown to anyone harbouring hopes of reunification just how far the games had diverged and how problematic any on-field reconciliation would be. Despite the difficulties, hopes of reunification remained alive, various people advancing timetables stretching from five to 20 years hence. However, most of those timetables took no account of the politics involved.

The most important outcome was that rugby league's days as an outlaw game were finally over and it was recognised as one of the twin souls of the rugby game. Thanks to Wigan's performances during May, recognition of the skills and pace of league's players was no longer generally confined to the north of England. Suddenly the rest of English rugby had woken up to the qualities inherent in league. Rugby union, after publicly denying itself such forbidden fruit for a century, suddenly wanted to know more and eagerly set about gaining insights into league methods. Further law changes to allow union to serve up the kind of attacking play that was on offer in league matches started to be discussed.

As the days of summer lengthened, English rugby, after 100 years of conflict, finally found itself formally at peace. Undoubtedly, summer 1996 marked the start of something new and expectations were high, but no one within rugby league was really sure whether it would be another short-term convergence or the start of something closer and more lasting. After a century of separation, the future of English rugby was once more in a state of flux. What, everyone involved with rugby league wondered, would the next few years bring?

Part Two: The modern era

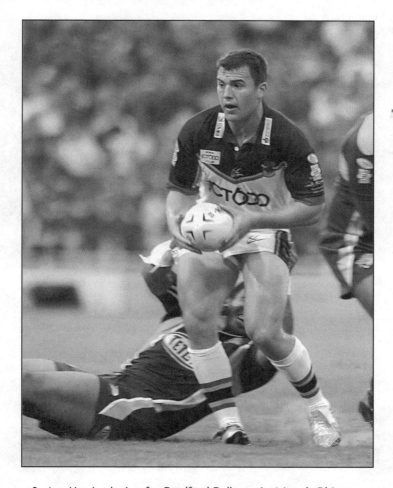

Iestyn Harris playing for Bradford Bulls against Leeds Rhinos.
Harris is the most prominent player to have played professional
rugby league, then professional rugby union (for Cardiff and Wales),
and then returned to top flight rugby league.
(Photo: David Williams)

Representatives of 2005 junior rugby league in London.
(Photo: Peter Lush)

Amateur rugby league: The West Indies squad from the 2004 Middlesex
Nines competition, organised by London Skolars.
(Photo: Peter Lush)

3. Rugby league: London and the South

In March 1995, rugby league in London and the south had a presence, but could hardly be said to be thriving. Ten years on, the game is vastly stronger, and has set down roots in areas that had hardly heard of the game in 1995.

The London Broncos were playing at Copthall Stadium in Barnet in the Second Division. The London Amateur League was playing on Sunday mornings, and while keeping the amateur game alive, was not as strong as in the past. The game was played in some schools and colleges, but did not have a widespread presence.

Since leaving Craven Cottage in 1984, and breaking with Fulham FC, Fulham (subsequently the London Crusaders and from 1994 the London Broncos) had come close to closure at least three times due to financial problems, but had survived. The most recent crisis had been during the previous season. New owners had assembled an expensive team, including former rugby union All Black and Londoner John Gallagher and former New Zealand rugby league captain Sam Stewart. While the team had played wonderful attacking rugby on the pitch, and missed promotion to the First Division by a point; off the pitch it had taken the intervention of the Rugby Football League to keep the club going after the new owners had effectively disappeared three months into the season.

Various consortiums were interested in buying the club, but there was still considerable surprise among the club's fans when it was announced that the Brisbane Broncos had purchased the club in February 1994. They saw it as a commercial opportunity to apply the lessons they had learnt in Brisbane in a new city, and planned to use the club as a nursery to develop young Brisbane players. Reinforcements had arrived, on the pitch in the form of Leo Dynevor and Victor Timms, and off the pitch in Robbie Moore, who took over running the club. Popular Kiwi coach Tony Gordon left at the end of the season, and was replaced by Gary Greinke, who had played in Britain, but did not have a great deal of top level coaching experience.

For the 1994-95 season, the Crusaders became the Broncos, and the club bought over more Brisbane players, but the combination of many of Gordon's team and the new imports never really gelled. Greinke's cautious approach alienated many of the fans, and the team was destined to miss out on promotion.

The question of a "Super League" had been mentioned in various places prior to the shock announcement of the game's new structure in April 1995. It is not unreasonable to assume that the Brisbane Broncos were aware of the prospect of Super League, and that a team in London would be a likely part of the new structure.

Did London deserve promotion at the end of the 1994-95 season? On the pitch, the simple answer is no. The team was not good enough. The Brisbane Broncos had under-estimated the quality of the British Second Division, with some of the players they brought over not really good enough, and Greinke's coaching had been unimaginative.

However, for the new Super League to have credibility as a new competition, with a more national, if not European base, it was essential that London were in the top flight, otherwise Super League would have been the old First Division with a different label, but played in summer.

London struggled through the game's final winter professional season, playing in the top flight, with various reinforcements coming from Australia, and home games played on a variety of grounds, including Harlequins' The Stoop. This in itself was a major indicator of the new relationship between the codes, now professional rugby league was being played at a top-flight rugby union club. The Broncos fans were shocked by how basic the facilities were at the Stoop, before the wholesale redevelopment that has produced the modern, compact stadium of today. And the club came close to collapse – again – when the Brisbane Broncos decided that their London adventure was costing too much, and pulled the plug. But Barry Maranta saved the day, and the credibility of Super League, by selling his Brisbane shares and taking ownership of the club.

Space does not allow for a detailed analysis of the Broncos' performances in Super League. Gary Greinke, much to the fans' relief, was sacked just before the new competition was launched, and former Leeds centre Australian Tony Currie was appointed as coach. London's home debut was at a new home – Charlton FC's The Valley in south east London. Their opponents were Paris St Germain. Supported by widespread publicity in the Murdoch-owned press, crowds flocked to the game, queuing round the ground to get in. From less than 1,000 watching Second Division matches at Copthall in 1994-95, over 9,000 were watching Super League a year later. It was a wonderful occasion, London winning 38-22. Although the crowds did not quite match this level again, a basis of support was built for the team in the area. London finished fourth in Super League, and although the team was largely Australian, important work was also done with a new youth structure, headed by Bev Risman, and in local schools. And in August, the shrewd signing of Martin Offiah from Wigan gave the team a player who people in the capital had actually heard of – and a Londoner as well!

Barry Maranta deserves huge credit for his work in building the London Broncos. But, with the benefit of hindsight, moving from The Valley to share at The Stoop for the 1997 season was a mistake. One of the perennial problems in London that people not familiar with the capital do not always appreciate is that it is a vast area, and travelling from one part to another is not always simple. For a newly converted supporter from the Charlton area to travel to matches at The Stoop in Twickenham involved a round trip of over two-and-a-half hours, whether by public transport or car. Not surprisingly, many of the new supporters were lost.

The 1997 season, despite the move, was one of the most memorable in the club's history. The team finished runners-up in Super League, playing some wonderful rugby. But perhaps the most memorable matches were in the World Club Challenge. This competition, including the Super League clubs from Europe and down under, was a disaster for most of the European teams. It exposed the vast gulf between the two competitions, and some results were embarrassing for the English clubs.

However, London sports followers love a big occasion. The visit of teams such as Brisbane and Canberra to The Stoop attracted near capacity crowds. That they were played on warm summer evenings, with few counter-attractions, helped as well. And the Broncos' 38-18 victory over the Canberra raiders, after being 14-0 down early on, was particularly memorable.

But at the end of the season, Barry Maranta decided to return home to Australia. Richard Branson had become interested in rugby league, and had become a minority shareholder in the club. He bought Maranta's shares, and suddenly the Broncos were part of the Virgin Group.

While this gave the club some financial stability, the loss of Maranta's hands-on day-to-day management was a major one. Virgin never seemed to have a clear idea how to develop the club. The 1997 team broke up, with some players returning to Australia, and not being replaced by players of the same quality. One major signing from Australia, prop forward Mark Carroll, never settled in London and only lasted one season. And at the end of the 1998 season, Tony Currie was sacked.

The 1999 season was full of contrasts. Currie's replacement, Dan Stains, was clearly not of the same quality, and was sacked in June after a particularly woeful performance at Bradford. But, with the fortune of a favourable draw, and magnificent semi-final win over Castleford, he had taken the team to the Challenge Cup Final at Wembley. It was the last rugby league match at the 'old' stadium, and 13,000 London supporters rallied behind the team. One group toured the teams' former grounds on their way to the match. Once again, the massive support for the team showed the potential for the game in London. With 20 minutes left, London were 20-16 down to Leeds Rhinos. But in the Wembley heat, Leeds ran away with the match, winning 52-16.

Meanwhile, crowds were declining at The Stoop. So at the end of the season, the club moved back across London to The Valley. For such a move to be successful, a competitive team – at least at home – is essential. But the Broncos struggled under new coach John Monie, who could not repeat in London his previous record as one of the game's most successful coaches at Wigan and in Australia. The club celebrated their 20th anniversary on 25 June, when Wigan, their first opponents at Craven Cottage in 1980, visited The Valley. Monie was unlucky with injuries, with

Shaun Edwards retiring, and Brendan Magnus, his alternative at scrum-half, also being released after a serious injury. Monie was sacked before the end of the season.

For the 2001 season, Tony Rea made the unusual move from chief executive to first team coach. He was replaced as chief executive by Lionel Hurst, a long-time rugby league activist and one of the driving forces behind the formation of the Rugby League Conference. New recruits strengthened the team, but towards the end of the season, the club once again faced a crisis when Virgin announced that their support for the club was going to end. Once again, it looked as if professional rugby league in London could collapse, particularly when Charlton FC announced that the Valley would not be available to the Broncos for 2002.

The crisis was resolved through David Hughes, a Charlton FC director, who had become a minority shareholder in the club, buying the Virgin Group's shares. Lionel Hurst left and was replaced as chief executive by Nic Cartwright, and the club moved back to west London, settling at Brentford FC's homely Griffin Park. While The Valley had been fine in 1996, by 2000, the ground had been further developed, and for most matches, only the main stand was used, meaning the play took place with a backdrop of thousands of empty seats. Griffin Park, with a capacity of around 10,000, gave a better atmosphere for the usual crowds of between 3,000 and 5,000.

The crisis of 2001 also restored some of the community spirit among supporters that had sustained the club in the second half of the 1980s at Chiswick. While Virgin were in control, there was little incentive for fans to fund raise and take other initiatives to help the club. A Supporters Action Group grew out of the 2001 crisis, and anyone attending a match at Griffin Park in 2005 was bombarded by volunteers selling raffle tickets, running stalls and helping with other activities on match days.

The focus of the club's playing strength has varied, between Australians and bringing players down from the game's northern heartlands. It is interesting how some players are more willing to travel across the world to play in London, while others are reluctant to move 250 miles. The recruitment of younger British players, who have settled in London, such as Paul Sykes, Rob Purdham and Neil Budworth, has given the team a more consistent composition. However, a legitimate criticism of the club is that they have failed to develop young Londoners to the top level. Joe Mbu, now fully established in the first team squad, shows the potential that exists. The club were unfortunate to lose Londoner Dominic Peters to a drugs ban, after he had become a regular first team player. Some of the Broncos former Academy players have continued in the professional game with the London Skolars, and others have played for National League clubs in the north. However, it is frustrating for Broncos fans to see a player such as northern youngster Peter Lupton established in the Hull first team squad, when he was never given many opportunities

London Skolars versus York City Knights –
LHF National League Two action June 2005. (Photo: Peter Lush)

Rugby League Conference Grand Final 2004:
Widnes Saints versus West London Sharks at St Albans (Photo: Peter Lush)

2000 Rugby World Cup launch at Rugby School: Great Britain veterans against an international selection. (Photo: Peter Lush)

Martin Offiah – the greatest ever Londoner
to play rugby league.
(Photo: Peter Lush)

in his time with the Broncos. The club have tried to resolve the problem of developing young players without running an under-21 side by loaning players to other clubs for their academy teams. Hopefully this will see more Londoners in the Broncos' first team in the future.

Since moving back to Griffin Park, the club's fortunes have been uneven. Reaching the play-offs in 2003 was followed by a struggle against relegation in 2004. But as the club moves towards its 25th anniversary, and has survived another financial crisis at the start of the 2005 season, surely it is time that some supporters in the north stopped questioning whether we need a club in London. If the game is going to develop at schools, youth and amateur levels, a professional club at the top level as a target for those young players to aspire to is essential. How many more Martin Offiahs – or Joe Mbus – are there in London waiting to play rugby league?

The Broncos have worked consistently in schools, and the results of this work are seen at every home game, as two teams of under-eight 'half-time heroes' from local schools play tag rugby. In 2004, 1,500 local school students received rugby league coaching through the Broncos' community work. The club is also work with Brentford FC in local education programmes based at Griffin Park, and have organised rugby league festivals and summer camps. In 2005, young players in London were given free match tickets to Broncos home games, again stressing the importance of playing at junior level and a local Super League club. In 2000 and 2001, local development work initiated by the Broncos resulted in the formation of the Greenwich Admirals, who are still competing in the Rugby League Conference, ensuring league retained a presence in south east London when the Broncos left the area.

However, towards the end of the 2005 season, there was another twist in the development of rugby league in London. A move back to The Stoop was announced, with a close collaboration with Harlequins RFC. This move included abandoning the 'Broncos' name in favour of 'Harlequins', meaning that "Come on you Quins" will be heard at rugby league matches. Compared to before August 1995, the rugby world has, indeed, turned upside down. If this move, combined with the recruitment of Ian Lenagan as club chairman, means that additional funding will be available to promote the club, then the move should be beneficial to the future of Super League in London. It will also mean an end to the long mid-season break at Griffin Park, which can only be a positive development.

The London Skolars

In 1995, London could barely support one professional club. Now there are two. The Skolars can claim to be unique – the only professional club in the modern era to have developed from an amateur club. Founded in

1995 as Student Rugby League Old Boys, with the aim of keeping former student players involved in the game, they started life playing on park pitches in east London.

One problem rugby league faced until the development of the Rugby League Conference and National League Three was how to fit new, aspiring clubs from outside the heartlands into the game's structures. The Skolars did play at one time in the BARLA National Conference, but found the continual trips 'up north' for away matches every other week impossible to sustain for an amateur team. A few years earlier, Hemel Hempstead had faced exactly the same problem. The Skolars found a home in the Rugby League Conference, and as the club's structure developed under the direction of chairman Hector McNeil, moved towards entering the professional game. In 2003, they became members of National League Two, making their debut against Dewsbury in the Arriva Trains Cup in January 2003.

The Skolars were determined not to make the mistake other new entrants to the professional game made, and vastly over-estimate their potential support. They budgeted for gates of 250, which meant a conservative budget for spending on players. This meant a struggle on the pitch in the first season, but ensured the club's survival. The first win, against Gateshead in August 2003, followed a draw at York in May. While the team finished bottom of the league, they had established a reputation as a well-run operation. The team was strengthened by new recruits in 2004, inevitably including some new Australians. This made the team a far more potent force on the pitch, and saw some credible victories. What was also encouraging was to see a number of former Broncos Academy players now having the opportunity to continue in the professional game, and not being lost to rugby union, their only option for playing at a reasonable level and staying in the south.

In 2005, the Skolars have not been as successful in National League Two (at the time of writing) as in 2004. The proposal to have a full-time coach in 2006 should help develop the club's players, and ensure that success on the pitch is linked to their work off it.

The Skolars also deserve enormous credit for their development work. Even before the club entered the professional ranks, it employed a local development officer. The club retains its links to the amateur game with their 'A' team playing in the Rugby League Conference, and in 2004 set up another local side, Haringey Hornets. They competed initially in the London Amateur League, but for 2005 entered the rugby league conference. The Hornets also run three junior teams.

Amateurs and schools

In 1995, the London Amateur League, which has a history going back to the mid-1960s, was an established part of the amateur rugby league set-up, but playing on Sunday mornings in winter restricted its potential for development.

The launch of the Southern Conference League in 1997, played in summer, with unrestricted use of rugby union grounds and players, transformed the amateur game outside league's traditional areas. BARLA had supported some pioneering work in various places outside the game's traditional areas in the 1980s, but it had often been difficult to sustain these clubs. But with the support of the RFL, the Rugby League Conference has taken the game into areas where it had barely been thought about before. Thetford, Bedford, St Albans and Cambridge are not places usually associated with rugby league, but the game has become established there due to the Rugby League Conference.

In London, teams such as West London and South London Storm have established a strong local presence, and established an historical first in 2005, when they became the first two London teams to meet in the Challenge Cup. West London were runners up in the RLC in 2004, losing in the final to an experienced Widnes side. South London Storm have created a thriving junior set-up, and won the Active Sports Club of the Year for London in 2004.

Eighteen teams from the south have competed in the Rugby League Conference up to 2004, and while there have been occasional collapses of clubs, most have been established on a firm foundation. Some, such as St Albans, Essex Eels and Hemel Stags have gone on to play in the newly created National League Three.

The London Amateur League has also switched to a summer playing season, and has effectively become a feeder league to the Rugby League Conference, allowing new clubs to find their feet in a less pressured environment before deciding whether they want to move up to the more testing Rugby League Conference.

The links between the professional and amateur game are very clear, with 17 of the Broncos' under-16 squad coming from amateur clubs in the London area. There are now eight RFL staff working on development in London, and the game at junior and schools level is now well-established. It has even reached some unlikely places. A team from Feltham Young Offenders Institution compete in the London Amateur League.

The game has also developed a 'service area' structure in London and the south east. Representative teams at under-14 and under-16 levels from four areas in London, and Hertfordshire, Essex and Surrey give opportunities for players to move towards national training camps and squads at different age levels.

In 2004, 151 schools from the south entered the Powergen Champion Schools competition, and this grew to 168 in 2005. The finals were held at Woollams, the base of NL3 side St Albans. Schools competing included The Coopers Company & Coburn, and King House, where Lawrence Dallaglio learnt his rugby. In 2005, new entrants included the prestigious

Whitgift School from Croydon. In 2003, only 50 schools entered, so there has clearly been a huge surge of interest in the sport, with over 80 percent of participants not having played before.

At national under-19 level, the London Leisure College, based in Greenwich, with a team including many players linked to the London Broncos, won the national under-19 student cup in 2003 and 2004. At Southgate College, the London Skolars have worked with the college to promote a rugby league study scheme for students, and similar work has been done at Isleworth College in west London.

In 2005, there were 46 junior teams being run by clubs in London and the South East. There were also five festivals organised. Combined with the activity in schools, there are now widespread opportunities for youngsters to play the game in London.

The game has also run education programmes for new coaches and referees, realising the importance of developing these areas of the game as well as encouraging new players.

Wales

Rugby league has longstanding links with Wales, but has always struggled to put down roots in the country. Various attempts have been made to establish professional clubs there, but these have failed through lack of support, with the hostility of the rugby union authorities not helping.

Once again, the new relationship between league and union, and the switch to the summer has created new opportunities for league in Wales. But, sadly, the game failed to capitalise on the impact of the 1995 Rugby League World Cup.

Wales had to argue with the game's leadership even to be able to enter the tournament, rather than a Great Britain team being the home nations' sole representative. But once the game's authorities accepted that a Wales team should play, the team made an enormous impact. This was helped by the rugby union team being at a low ebb, and the league team being built around various former union stars who had 'gone north'.

Led by Jonathan Davies, and including such notable stars as David Young, Kevin Ellis, John Devereux, Adrian Hadley, Antony Sullivan and a young Iestyn Harris, Wales opened the campaign with victory over France at Cardiff City's Ninian Park ground. This was followed by a 22-10 victory over Western Samoa at Swansea in what was regarded as the toughest – and possibly the best – game of an excellent tournament. Wales took 7,000 supporters to the semi-final at Old Trafford, but could not overcome England, who were helped by a Martin Offiah try which probably would have been disallowed had the 'video referee' facility been available.

Super League missed a wonderful opportunity for the game by not having a South Wales team in the new competition. A team based around the world cup team, involving Jonathan Davies either on or off the pitch, and based in Cardiff or Swansea, with the top clubs visiting the Principality, would have attracted widespread support. Instead, a South Wales team played in the Second Division. When a Super League match was staged in Wales, it attracted a good crowd, but the South Wales team was not well supported. The game's supporters in Wales, and rugby supporters in general, follow league closely on SKY television, and were well aware of the difference between the Second Division and Super League.

The game's authorities then refused the new club entry into Super League in 1997. A place in the First Division was apparently made available, but the club's officials and backers felt that only a Super League place would be viable, and the club collapsed.

Since then, there has been a growth in rugby league at grassroots level. Initially based in the colleges, this then developed into an open-age amateur side in Cardiff competing in the Rugby League Conference, and a Wales Division of the Conference in 2003. Most of the clubs in this division had close links to rugby union clubs, with the matches being played at grounds often of a higher standard than elsewhere in the conference. The playing standard was high as well, with former professionals, such as Kevin Ellis and John Devereux, turning out for Bridgend Blue Bulls. Both players were still playing club rugby union, and even made a return to the Wales rugby league team. With Bridgend now playing in National League Three, and the acceptance of the club, as the Celtic Crusaders, moving into the semi-professional National League Two in 2006, the game is probably stronger now in Wales than for many years. The prospect of a club based in South Wales in Super League is once again on the agenda.

One spin-off of rugby union going open is that the flow of union players into rugby league at the top level has dried up. The Welsh team has continued to play, but has not reached the same standards as in the past, although players are starting to come into professional rugby league from the student and amateur games. However, if the trends of the past five years continue, league can be optimistic about its future in Wales. As the game develops, more players will reach professional level, either in Wales or elsewhere, and the national side will rebuild again. Pride in the jersey is still there, as anyone who saw Wales' heroic performance at Huddersfield against Australia in the 2000 World Cup will testify. Coming the day after England had been overwhelmed 49-6 in their semi-final against New Zealand, Wales shocked the world champions by leading 20-14 at half-time, before losing 46-22.

In Scotland and Ireland, Rugby League Conferences being played in the summer has seen the base for the sport grow in both countries. Both now field a national team, and although supplemented by second and third generation Australian exiles in the 2000 World Cup, do have a genuine base. Again, rugby league has only just started to develop its potential in both countries.

The future

The financial crisis that hit the Broncos at the start of the 2005 season, and the narrow vote by the other Super League clubs in favour of the club being allowed to continue in Super League was a shock to the game's supporters in London and elsewhere 'beyond the heartlands'. Since Fulham started in 1980, the game's authorities have never recognised or understood the problems of building professional clubs in a new area, and the enormous investment involved. The game cannot afford to rely on a handful of rich individuals or corporations for its future in London. If rugby league really aspires to become a national sport, it must give financial and practical support to professional clubs beyond the heartlands in areas such as marketing and promotion. It also needs to recognise the higher cost of living in London in the salary cap and other staffing costs. Most salaried jobs in London have a 'London Weighting' element reflecting the higher cost of living in the capital; this should be reflected in the salary cap as well.

It also seems that the original development impetus when Super League was set up has been lost. With no disrespect to Leigh, who have a long rugby league tradition, does the game overall gain from that club joining Super League when there are already four other Super League clubs within easy travelling distance of the town? Wouldn't Super League clubs in South Wales and Dublin add to the game's profile, given that league is already widely followed on television in both areas, and is now establishing a playing base.

Surely it should not have been a choice between Coventry and Bridgend for a place in National League Two. Both had a valid case and would add to the game's national profile. The game's work in grassroots development has improved enormously over the past 10 years, but development at professional and grassroots go hand-in-hand.

The sport also has to consider carefully development at senior amateur level. National League Three has been very exciting, but can a league that includes travelling from Essex to Gateshead continue as an amateur competition? The withdrawal of Carlisle and Birmingham early in the 2005 season was a warning sign. There is a need for elite competitions, but maybe a degree of regionalisation, as in semi-professional association football, is necessary for the structure to develop solid foundations.

The number of 'southerners' who have come through amateur or schools structures into the professional game is slowly increasing. There is enthusiasm for rugby league when it is provided for young players. The question facing the game for the next 10 years is whether its leaders can grasp all the opportunities that will arise.

4. Professional rugby league since 1996

There is little doubt that the period since April 1995 has been one of the most important in the history of rugby league in Britain. The introduction of Super League has seen the sport at the top level become a full-time professional one, with a summer season. The professional game below Super League has also switched to summer, but stayed part-time.

The issues around the launch of Super League and the controversial proposed mergers of clubs initially put forward in 1995 have been covered in other books and this chapter will not go over that debate again. There is a compelling argument that the game needed a new image and direction. Despite various attempts to establish new clubs in the 1980s following the launch of Fulham, the London Broncos were the only professional club outside the game's heartlands, although the Sheffield Eagles had established the professional game in South Yorkshire.

Developments in rugby union cannot be ignored when considering the last 10 years in rugby league. A major factor behind the launch of Super League was coverage of rugby league on television in Australia, and a battle between competing media interests. But rugby union, despite its official 'amateur' status was facing exactly the same issues. With the development of its World Cup, and in Britain the growth of its league and cup competitions, combined with the Five Nations tournament, it had also become a major prize in the ever-competitive world of television rights.

From a rugby union point of view, the proposed launch of Super League in Australia raised the prospect of even more union players being drawn towards league because of the enormous financial rewards on offer. Thus, there was very strong pressure on union in the southern hemisphere in the spring of 1995 to go openly professional at the top level.

But from a rugby league standpoint, the reverse argument also applies. The "what if" approach to history should always be handled cautiously. But what if rugby league had stayed predominantly part-time at the top level – and in 1995 only the Wigan and Leeds clubs were in practice full-time – and rugby union had gone professional? There is a strong case for saying that given the commercial success of the 1995 Rugby Union World Cup, union would have gone professional at the top level by the year 2000, whatever happened in rugby league. This would have left rugby league even more vulnerable to having its best players poached by rugby union. Rugby league followers have seen Jason Robinson, Henry Paul, Iestyn Harris (for three years) and now Andy Farrell go to union, along with other former union players returning to their original code. There has not been a huge influx of league players to union, as some rugby union commentators gleefully anticipated. But what if rugby league was still predominantly part-time, and mainly based in the north of England? Any top class sportsman aspires to play sport full-time and inevitably for some league players this would have meant moving to union. League could have ended up isolated as a minor sport in the north of England, developing players for rugby union. At least the introduction of Super League avoided that fate.

So after almost 10 years of Super League, what is the state of professional rugby league in Great Britain? Has the game sold its soul for television money and abandoned its traditions? Or does it now have a strong commercially viable competition at the top level? The truth is probably somewhere between those two views.

It is clear that by going full-time, there has been a development in playing standards. Players today are fitter and more athletic, the game is faster (although some would argue that this is not necessarily a good development) and often provides a high level of entertainment. The academy structure has also meant that there is a clear path for young players to develop in the sport.

Part of the Super League ethos was to develop the marketing and profile of the game. This has been successful, with greater sponsorship, a more professional commercial approach by clubs, better community work and a higher profile. However, some of the initiatives in the early days of Super League, such as very loud music at matches, and pop music bands playing at half-time and before games were not generally successful. It was ironic that many of the ideas that were adopted by Super League, in particular the Bradford Bulls, were initially 'road-tested' by Keighley Cougars prior to the formation of Super League. Their dynamic marketing, adopting of a new nickname and mascot, and community initiatives all helped increase attendances dramatically, linked to success on the pitch. Yet the club were refused a place in Super League, for them the bitterest outcome of the changes to the game in 1995.

The original concept of Super League was of an international club competition with the top four European clubs playing the top four in Australia. The legal battles over Super League in Australia meant no international club matches took place in 1996. In 1997, a complex World Club Championship was played, involving all the Super League clubs in Europe and Australia. Overwhelmingly this was dominated by the Australian clubs, and was not seen as a great success. Matches were not particularly well attended, except in London, when it became clear that the Australian sides were dominating the tournament. For the London Broncos, the matches attracted good crowds, and a memorable victory over the Canberra Raiders.

This competition was not repeated, but in 2000, the World Club Challenge was revived, with the British champions facing their counterparts from Australia. Although in the first match Melbourne Storm beat St Helens 44-6, since then most matches have been closer, with some thrilling wins for the British sides. So far all the matches have been played in Great Britain – it would be a progressive development for the match to be played in Australia every other year.

The big four

Rugby league from the late 1980s to 1995 was dominated by Wigan. Since the start of Super League, Bradford Bulls, Leeds Rhinos, St Helens and Wigan Warriors have dominated the competition. No other club has won the competition, or even reached the Grand Final. St Helens have won the competition four times, Bradford Bulls on three occasions, and Wigan and Leeds Rhinos once each.

The domination by the 'big four' is also shown by the number of times they have lost to other clubs (i.e. not to each other):

Number of defeats to other clubs 1996 to 2004 (Nine seasons):

Club	Number of defeats	Average per season	Worst season
Bradford Bulls	19	2.11	7 defeats in 1998
Leeds Rhinos	32	3.56	10 defeats in 1996
St Helens	21	2.33	4 defeats in 1999 & 2004
Wigan Warriors	22	2.44	6 defeats in 1997

One of the successes of Super League has been the culmination of the season in the play-offs and Grand Final, which were introduced in 1998, replacing the end-of-season Premiership. In many ways, this is returning to the traditional end to the rugby league season, with the Championship Final that was the conclusion to the season for a long time. The play-offs have provided their own drama – Castleford's wonderful run in 1999 from fifth place to within a match of the Grand Final, and St Helen's last minute victory over Bradford in 2000.

The Grand Final as an occasion has developed well since 1998. Attendances have risen so that the match is now guaranteed to fill Old Trafford, using one of Great Britain's best sporting venues for the climax to the domestic club season.

Attendances as a measure of a competition's success are always subject to great debate. But some figures do show the progress that Super League and summer rugby league have made. Prior to Super League, the best average attendance in the top level since the re-introduction of two divisions was 7,292 in 1988-89. In the last conventional winter season, 1994-95, the average was 5,543. The 1995-96 Centenary Season was truncated and was regarded as a 'filler' before Super League started, but even that had an average attendance of 5,515.

The first season of Super League saw an immediate increase to 6,571. By the 2000 season, this had increased to 7,555, and by 2004 had

71

reached 8,833. In 1994-95, the top three club averages were: Wigan Warriors: 14,561, Leeds Rhinos: 12,516, St Helens: 7,467. The Bradford Bulls (then still known as Northern) were on 5,654. In 2004, Leeds Rhinos were top with 16,608, followed by Bradford on 13,500, Wigan on 13,333, Hull on 11,397 and Warrington just failing to reach five figures with 9,889. Despite having their worst season for years, which ended in relegation, Castleford Tigers averaged 7,035; a higher figure than they achieved in the 1980s or 1990s.

Another aspect of the game in which there has been enormous change since the introduction of Super League has been in the sport's grounds. Hull FC, Wigan and Warrington have all moved to modern, all-seater stadiums. Huddersfield had already achieved this prior to the start of Super League, and the Galpharm Stadium has become a regular venue for internationals and other major games. Their approach of sharing the stadium with the local football club was repeated at Hull and Wigan. While this has meant the loss of some of the sport's great venues, it has generally been reflected in greater attendances. Wigan are the exception to this, but that could also be because of the relative decline of the team's performances in comparison to other clubs in the Super League era, compared to their domination of the sport in the late 1980s and early 1990s. Even then, despite moving from Central Park, their 2004 average crowd of 13,333 was only just over 1,000 less than their average crowd from 1988 to 1994.

Of the clubs who have not moved, Widnes have stayed on the same site, but rebuilt their stadium completely to a compact, modern all-seater venue suitable for Super League. Bradford, Wakefield and Salford have all carried out some improvements, with the former being restricted for most of this period by uncertainty over the future of Odsal, with the club playing for two seasons at Bradford City FC's Valley Parade. Salford are now working towards moving to a new stadium. The London Broncos have had a somewhat nomadic existence during Super League, but have generally played at venues that are suitable for the modern era.

In the spring of 2005, the RFL published a report about the grounds of the National League One clubs, showing what work was required for them to be acceptable in Super League. Standards expected are clearly rising. For example, Castleford Tigers, despite nine years' membership of Super League, would be required to carry out improvements to their directors' box, toilets, floodlights, dug outs, access from the dressing room to the pitch, dressing rooms and television gantry and camera positions. Every club was required to carry out work to their floodlights. This may not seem surprising, but three of them play at Football League grounds (Doncaster, Oldham and Rochdale Hornets), and presumably their lights are acceptable to the Football League. Clubs were being given until 31 August 2005 to complete the work, which in reality, if this is applied strictly, would rule most of them out of contention for a Super League place in 2006.

Development

Super League's original vision was of a competition based in big cities, with an international pan-European dimension. Looking at the League in 2005, with 11 clubs out of 12 from the game's M62 corridor heartlands, including five concentrated in a relatively small area of Lancashire & Cheshire, it would be fair to say that the development side of Super League has failed so far. What went wrong?

The original 12 Super League clubs included two – Paris St Germain and London – which were beyond the heartlands, and Sheffield Eagles, who although within 40 miles of the M62, were not in a traditional rugby league area. Paris St Germain hosted the first Super League fixture, beating Sheffield Eagles 30-24 on 29 March 1996 in front of 17,873 enthusiastic fans in the Charlety Stadium. One of the highlights of the first Super League season was supporters' trips to follow their team to Paris – a glamorous change from hopping along a few junctions of the M62 or the annual trip 'down south' to London. But the club failed to build on a successful first season. Their second season saw the club field a team mainly made up of Australians with management support provided by the Rugby Football League. But attendances slumped, with only 500 attending the game against Salford, and just more than 1,000 against Castleford three days later. Paris St Germain avoided relegation, but the club withdrew from Super League with hopes of a later return, which has not materialised. In 2006, France will again return to Super League, with Les Catalans joining in 2006, and the possibility of a second French club when the competition expands to 14 clubs.

Super League's next expansion move was in 1999, when Gateshead Thunder entered the competition. The RFL had been using Gateshead Athletics Stadium as a venue for some big matches since the early 1990s, when the pre-season Charity Shield was staged there twice. A match in the 1995 World Cup was played in Gateshead, and the England international team had also played there. At local level, there had been successful development work, with amateur clubs, schools and students all playing the game.

Kath Hetherington and Australian Shane Richardson were the driving force behind the new club. The team was predominantly made up of Australians, and finished a creditable sixth in Super League, with 19 wins and a draw from 30 matches. Although they played a very regimented Australian style, they attracted average crowds of 3,895 – something to build on in the soccer-mad north east. However, the club hit financial problems, and instead of offering support, the RFL merged them with Hull FC, who were also in difficulties. In reality, although some of the

73

Gateshead players moved to Hull, this destroyed 10 years patient development work in the north east. After a year's break, local supporters reformed the club, who have played in the Northern Ford Premiership and then National League Division Two ever since. They have found it hard to attract support, although they deserve much credit for keeping the flame of professional rugby league alive in the north east.

At the same time, the game lost one of its surviving development clubs from Super League when Sheffield Eagles merged with the Huddersfield Giants. Sheffield's achievement in winning the Challenge Cup in 1998 is arguably one the sport's great moments, a team no-one fancied to beat the mighty Wigan doing so at Wembley. But the Eagles had failed to build on that success, and in some ways were handicapped by their stadium. The Don Valley stadium might be fine for athletics, but a crowd of even 5,000 seems lost in it for rugby league, with vast expanses of empty seats, and the supporters far from the pitch. Fulham and the London Crusaders had exactly the same experience at the Crystal Palace athletics stadium. Sheffield had played some matches at Sheffield United FC's Bramall Lane ground, and had looked towards a permanent move there.

As with Gateshead, all was not lost for professional rugby league in Sheffield, and Mark Aston revived the club who continued playing in the Northern Ford Premiership for the 2000 season. The merger was of little benefit to Huddersfield, who struggled in the 2000 season, trying to merge two squads of players with different backgrounds. Sheffield have stayed in the National League, with no immediate prospects of a return to Super League.

Another missed opportunity, covered elsewhere in this book, was with South Wales in 1996. The game had a very high standing following the 1995 World Cup and Wales' excellent performances. A team based around that side could have been competitive in Super League, but the opportunity to promote the South Wales club in 1996 into Super League was missed. But with the game getting stronger at amateur level and in the schools and colleges in South Wales, the entry of the ambitious Celtic Crusaders to NL2 in 2006, a move into Super League could follow in the future. Similarly, both Dublin and Glasgow have potential for Super League clubs in the future.

One initiative that Super League did take in 1998 was to play games 'On the Road', so that areas of the country (usually where amateur rugby league was played) could see a professional match 'live'. Thus, Gateshead, Northampton, Edinburgh, Cardiff and Swansea all staged matches. This initiative has not been repeated, although in 1999 Gateshead and London Broncos both staged matches away from their home base due to stadium unavailability, and both attracted good crowds. 'On the Road' games have become a regular feature of the London Broncos season, due to the need to reseed their pitch outside the football season, but the club have had problems finding venues to accommodate the matches, and thus at times not much promotion work for the game around these fixtures has been carried out. There was interest in the 1998 programme, and if linked with other development work, is something the game could consider again in the future.

Television

The growth of Super League has been inextricably linked to coverage on Sky Sports. This has even become part of the game itself, with video replays being used to help make decisions in matches covered by Sky. There can be little dispute that technically, Sky's coverage is very good, and has clearly pressured the BBC to improve their coverage of the Challenge Cup. It can also be argued that Sky's regular coverage, with two British and two Australian matches each week, plus a magazine programme, has helped spread interest in the game beyond its traditional areas. Access to satellite television channels has spread over the past 10 years, and it is unlikely that terrestrial television would ever have given this depth of coverage to the game.

The BBC has continued to cover the Challenge Cup, and has developed that to two matches over a Challenge Cup weekend. Its introduction of Clare Balding to host the programmes, whose genuine enthusiasm for the sport comes through all the time, has improved their presentation immeasurably. With the Challenge Cup Final moving to the end of August, hopefully the competition can be restored to its rightful and traditional high profile slot in the rugby league season, rather than the 'pre-season' feel the early rounds have had so far in the summer era, with the final being played in April or May.

However, it is very frustrating that the BBC refuses to show their highlights programme, the *Super League Show*, nationally. It is only shown in the north, to the frustration of rugby league fans elsewhere. Until they do this, and acknowledge that rugby league can genuinely claim to be a national sport, their coverage will always lack credibility compared to Sky. And for those who complain that Super League matches are only shown on Sky, not terrestrial channels, they should remember that viewers outside the north have never had league matches available to them on the terrestrial channels.

One area of continual frustration for followers of the game on television has been the lack of coverage of the National League. Sky now shows the Grand Finals live, but some regular coverage would be welcome. And it is disappointing that the terrestrial channels in the north do not show a highlights package. Prior to Super League, Sky's coverage had a little more flexibility, with, for example, London Crusaders versus Workington being shown in 1994 when both teams were battling for promotion from the Second Division. However, on the positive side, the student Varsity match has now become a regular live feature on Sky

75

Sports, and has been a success, even if not showing the sport's highest levels of skill and technique.

A further area of frustration for some fans is that the international matches are not screened live on terrestrial television, but restricted to highlights packages on Sunday afternoons. Apart from the loss of potential viewers, this has also meant matches being played at 6.15pm, not the most convenient time for supporters. While the coverage on Sky has been comprehensive and well presented, there is a feeling in the game that international matches on Saturday or Sunday afternoons would attract a larger audience either on Sky or particularly on terrestrial television.

A further problem for television viewers is that with Super League only having 12 clubs, a regular watcher who also attends their club's matches is seeing the same teams with monotonous regularity. Watching both live games at the weekend, and going to a match, means that the viewer has seen half of the teams in Super League. This is a further argument for live television coverage to break out of the Super League ghetto every-so-often.

Promotion and relegation

In May 2005 the RFL outlined a new strategy for Super League. Superficially, this was seen as abolishing promotion and relegation. The reality is more complex than that. The RFL have pointed out that there is no automatic promotion and relegation now, and indeed that has been the case since Super League started, with both Hunslet and Dewsbury not being promoted after winning the Northern Ford Premiership. There will also be pressure on existing Super League clubs to meet the criteria laid down for the competition, and some are falling short of that now.

What was announced by the RFL was an aim of expanding Super League to 14 clubs from 2009 and that new clubs were to be given guaranteed three-year tenure in the competition. However, the RFL have also said that new clubs in the United Kingdom would have to work their way up through the National Leagues.

In reality, there are only a relatively small number of the current National League clubs who have a structure and large enough catchment area to be viable in Super League. The RFL's new approach makes it clear what criteria are necessary to apply for Super League, and gives both existing clubs and potential new franchises a clear target to aim for. While a number of clubs fighting against relegation can be exciting, as in the 2004 season, it does not help the game if a club is automatically promoted to Super League without a structure and playing squad to be competitive at that level, and spend the next season struggling at the bottom of the league. The three year tenure approach should help overcome this problem. It was interesting that Steve Evans, the chairman of Featherstone Rovers, interviewed by *Rugby League World*, welcomed the new approach, saying: "We believe that the proposed strategy will reward clubs such as ours, and rather than closing the door to Super League it actually opens it wider for us." Given that Featherstone were opposed to the foundation of Super League, which effectively excluded them from the game's top flight, and have never played at that level, this is an enlightened attitude.

If the new structure means a wider geographical spread of clubs playing at the top level, that can only benefit the game. In development terms, the lessons of the last 25 years – since Fulham joined the RFL in 1980 – are that having a professional club and a thriving amateur and schools structure go together. The professional club will not develop without establishing roots in the area; the existence of the professional club gives young players something to strive towards. The seven and eight year-olds playing tag rugby at half-time in the London Broncos matches are the potential academy players in 10 years time and potential professional stars in 15 years time.

Below Super League

In common with both association football and rugby union, it would be fair to say that the gulf between the top flight of rugby league and the next tier down has widened immeasurably over the past 10 years.

Under the old First and Second Divisions, particularly when four clubs were promoted and relegated each season, it was not uncommon for clubs to 'yo-yo' between the two divisions. To a certain extent, that has happened in the Super League era, when clubs that have been relegated have maintained a full-time squad with the aim of returning immediately to the top level. If the criteria for membership of Super League are to be implemented more strictly in the future, that strategy may not be so simple, with work off the pitch as important as success on it.

In 1987-88, the average attendance in the Second Division was 1,364, less than 25 per cent of that in the First Division. In 1994-95, the figures were almost identical, with an increase of 4 in the Second Division figure, which was still just less than 25 per cent of the First Division's 5,543. Comparisons since then are difficult, as Super League is smaller than the old First Division, with clubs with higher attendances boosting the lower league's average. For example in 2000, the Northern Ford Premiership (NFP) average was 1,525, just over 20 per cent of Super League's 7,555. By 2004, the NFP had been split into National League One and National League Two. National League One's average was 1,482, below the NFP figure in 2000, and was only 16.7 per cent of Super League's 8,833. For National League Two, the average crowd was 726.

So there clearly has been a greater gap open up between Super League and the rest. This has been exacerbated by the cutting of money from the News Corporation sponsorship of the game for the National League clubs, although this has been replaced to a limited extent by new sponsorship for the National League. Also, when the game switched to a summer season, some of the then NFP clubs showed little enthusiasm for this move, and did little to adapt to the summer game. Indeed, around 2000 and 2001 they were almost reverting to a winter season, starting their league in December so as to be able to play competitive matches over the Christmas period.

However, there have also been positive developments. Some clubs have managed major improvements to their grounds, Batley being an outstanding example. Others have faced problems, such as Oldham who have experienced problems since leaving The Watersheddings, and Halifax, whose half-finished ground has become a millstone for both them and Halifax Football Club, although there are now plans to complete the building work.

Some clubs have been lost from the professional structure, such as Prescot and Bramley, although the latter reformed and now compete in the amateur National League Three. Another shock to the game came when York withdrew from the RFL in 2002 with major financial problems. The club had struggled since leaving their longstanding home in the centre of the city in the 1980s, moving to the Ryedale Stadium, which had poor public transport links. However, a new club was formed and re-entered the league in 2003 in National League Two. And in 2004, Chorley moved to Blackpool, becoming the Blackpool Panthers. This both returned the sport at a professional level to a town where it had first been played in the 1950s, but meant the loss of Chorley as a professional venue for the sport.

On a positive note, both the London Skolars and Gateshead Thunder have become established in National League Two. For the game to develop, it is important that the opportunity to play semi-professional rugby league is offered to clubs currently in National League Three, which has happened with Bridgend, as the Celtic Crusaders, moving into NL2 in 2006.

There is still further potential for development of the National League structure. The early-season National League Cup can provide some very ill-matched fixtures, with teams from the bottom of National League Two facing inevitable slaughters at the hands of strong National League One sides. The knock-out stages of this competition also case breaks in the fixtures for clubs who do not reach that stage. Maybe expanding the leagues and running this competition on a knock-out basis would be a solution.

Another area that the National Leagues could consider is some form of representative matches. A county championship, including an 'Other Nationalities' team made up of overseas players in the National League, could provide representative rugby for leading players, and help develop players for the Wales, Scotland and Ireland teams. Possibly a National League XIII could play representative teams from other countries, or tour abroad. All this would help raise the competition's profile, and if some matches were played midweek, could also attract supporters who normally follow Super League.

Rugby league's structure

It would be fair to say that the professional game went through some very difficult times in the period following the formation of Super League, when there was a feeling among supporters that it lacked a clear direction, and each section of the game was attempting to protect its own 'patch'. The formation of Super League (Europe) as a separate entity was followed by the formation of FASDA to represent the rest of the professional game. While these were theoretically only marketing organisations, the game appeared fragmented and to lack a clear direction. A turnover at the top of the game did not help, with various leaders arriving and departing with worrying regularity, and staff being made redundant by the RFL.

The appointment of Richard Lewis as executive chairman of the RFL in 2002, with a new board and the merging of various bodies back into the RFL has seen a welcome period of stability at the top of the game. As well as more consistency in the management of the professional game, the RFL and BARLA have managed to achieve unity, which has been crucial for the game's relationship with Sport England and other external bodies. That Sports Minister Richard Caborn could comment in the spring of 2005 that rugby league was a well-administered game was recognition of the progress that has been made.

The future

Some journalists, particularly those who write about rugby union, regularly write off rugby league, and seen it being subsumed into rugby union as inevitable. In fact, it can be argued that with the spread of the Rugby League Conference, and the strength of Super League, rugby league is in a strong position. Of course the game has weaknesses, but so does every professional sport. The standard of the professional game has improved over the past 10 years; fitness levels are higher, as are the players' skills. The international game is also improving with the World Club Challenge, Tri-nations tournament, and new countries taking up the game. The game's structure is stronger, with more consistent leadership.

Mistakes were made at the start of Super League, and it took time to overcome them. But if the game continues to look outwards, and recognise the importance of development at every level, than it can be confident of a secure future.

Super League action: 2005 London Broncos versus Hull at Bridgend.
(Photo: Peter Lush)

Castleford Tigers versus Whitehaven – 2005 Northern Rail Cup semi-final.
(Photo: Peter Lush)

5. Professional rugby union since 1996

In the minds of those rugby followers that are beyond the first flush of youth, rugby union will always be perceived as a game based on social connections rather than competitions. It was taken as read that the former guaranteed a club's standing in the game and that brought in its wake the most desirable fixtures and ensured access to the best players. Since the end of the 1970s that situation has been reversing bit-by-bit as competitions have come to the fore at the game's top level. Along the way, the amateur old guard has gradually ceded power until control has finally passed into the hands of a new group of professionally minded administrators and players. Even today, this development has not been universally welcomed and the administration of the English game at elite level is still bedevilled by a number of ongoing feuds.

The Guinness Premiership, which kicks off in September 2005, is the elite tier of English rugby union's club competitions and is the direct successor to the Allied Dunbar and Zurich Premierships. A change of sponsor is effectively the only difference for an organisation that has overtaken the knock-out cup to become England's primary competition. In doing so, it has played a key role in harnessing rugby union's rising popularity and boosting its commercial standing. While harsh economic circumstances pulled the Premiership's membership down from 14 to the current 12 in 1999, those remaining have ensured that well paid full-time professionalism has flourished, greatly increased the number of players imported from overseas and pushed the playing standards up to a much higher level. To cope with the growing spectator numbers, half of the members have had to set up some form of ground sharing arrangement with a neighbouring association football club. In a decade, the Premiership has grown a long way beyond the seamless league structure envisaged 20 years earlier.

Although relatively small, its 12 members manage to represent a number of cities and large towns across England, giving the Premiership a national spread. The majority are traditional pillars of the game in their locality, although in quite a few cases the old club has undergone a major revamp to meet the demands of the new era. Newcastle Falcons, Leeds Tykes and Sale Sharks represent the Premiership in the North. Bath, Bristol Shoguns and Gloucester make up the western contingent. Leicester Tigers, Northampton Saints and Worcester Warriors comprise the Midlands' membership. In the south-east, London Irish, London Wasps and Saracens fly the flag, although none of them do so any longer within Greater London itself.

With every member of the Premiership having the opportunity to participate in one of the three European club competitions held each season and the Powergen English Cup, the fixture programme has become very congested and as a result highly structured. With the various England teams also having extensive fixture lists, it has made the possibility of club versus country conflicts over player availability much higher as the two bodies lay claim to as many weeks of the season as they can. To accommodate the multiplicity of demands, Premiership matches have had to be played on international weekends, an arrangement which has led the richer clubs to build bigger squads in a bid to protect themselves against unexpected defeats due to the absence of key players on international duty.

Both sides know they are heavily reliant on each other; the national team being almost exclusively dependent on the talent contracted to Premiership clubs, the Premiership recognising that it is the main beneficiary of a successful national side. Tension will always be present, but it is heightened on occasions when the RFU attempts to set the agenda unilaterally by imposing conditions on the central funding it distributes under an eight year agreement reached in 2001. Being in a position to hand over annually around £2,000,000 to each club, plus £30,000 compensation for every player called into the national squad, undoubtedly puts the national body in a very strong negotiating position.

At various times those negotiations have turned sour and led to calls for the England squad members to be centrally contracted to the national Union, as is the case in Ireland. Only fears that central contracts might in the long-term prove counter-productive has blocked the progress of this contentious option on a number of occasions.

Fixture congestion has not prevented European competition being embraced after a hesitant start. With stunningly bad timing, proposals for a European Cup reached the RFU in April 1995, when fear of promoters was rife. At a time of great uncertainty and doubt, the RFU refused to permit its leading clubs to enter the competition when it was launched at in 1995. Their fears allayed, the RFU granted permission for the following season, 1996-97, but problems over fixture scheduling surfaced and led the English clubs to boycott the Cup in 1998-99. It took less than 12 months for the fixture issues to be resolved and since then six Premiership clubs have had the right to enter the hugely successful Heineken Cup, while the other six are split between the less prestigious European Challenge Cup and the European Shield. All the major European Unions are fully committed to those competitions, which are recognised as being a step up from the domestic league competitions. Although it has become almost totally restricted to English and French clubs, the Heineken Cup Final, now settled in an end-of-season slot, is recognised as the European club game's great finale.

With so many competitions all ending in a play-off, the end of season has become extremely busy. In addition to the three European finals, which might involve English clubs, a play-off was introduced involving a semi-final and a Twickenham final to decide the Premiership's champion

82

club. There is also a wildcard play-off for the clubs in the lower sections of the Premiership, again culminating in a final at Twickenham, which offers a lucrative place in the Heineken Cup. While many have questioned the validity of the whole play-off concept, it does provide a way for even more revenue to be generated, particularly for those clubs that are in form at the end of the season.

Leicester Tigers are one of those top clubs and claim to be the most popular rugby club in England, a claim that could be disputed by Leeds Rhinos. Certainly the Tigers are undoubtedly the most popular rugby union club in the country and it is their commercial strength that sets the yardstick for the rest of the Premiership. The cost of competing with the Tigers for Premiership success can be extremely high and in some cases almost ruinous for a club without a good fan-base or the support of a major investor. Losing Premiership status can be catastrophic financially and on a number of occasions Premier Rugby Ltd, which represents the clubs involved, has raised the desirability of ending promotion from and relegation to the National League in favour of some form of franchise system to offset the problems.

For some clubs, the advent of open professionalism opened up a harsh decade of rationalisation with hardly any concessions to tradition. First to go from the elite were those northern clubs, like Orrell and West Hartlepool, whose mix of locally produced talent, volunteer labour and a small loyal crowd no longer provided the resources necessary for their survival. For others, like the Bedford Blues, the loss of a major investor marked the end of their hopes of Premiership success. They were not the only ones unable to maintain their challenge in the new environment. So far, of those relegated and subsequently pushed to the verge of liquidation only Bristol has managed to claw its way back into the elite.

Linked to, but very separate from the elite in the Guinness Premiership, are the not so elite National Leagues – organised in four divisions, One, Two and Three (North and South). What separates them these days is not so much a gap as a chasm. Now that the 12 Premiership clubs do not have to enter the Powergen Cup until the round of the last 16 there is very little chance of a member of the National Leagues even meeting an elite club in a competitive match.

Without a sponsor and seemingly unloved, the National Leagues struggle to maintain ambition in very unequal circumstances. While a member of National One receives about a tenth of what a Premiership club receives from RFU central funds, it has to try and compete with a recently relegated club for the one promotion place. They hardly meet on a level playing field as the recently relegated club has been compensated for that misfortune with a one-off payment of £750,000, or if it happened to be a founder member of the Premiership, such as Harlequins, of £1,800,000. Unless the National One club has major backers, it cannot be expected to gain promotion, a situation that helps to sustain accusations that the Premiership is a closed shop. Further backing for those accusations is provided by the minimum ground standards that have to be met before any club can be promoted.

The National Leagues comprise a wide mix of clubs – a few very ambitious ones maintaining some full-time professionals in the hope of an imminent move upwards, while the vast majority operate on a part-time basis with their players holding on to some form of day job. Amongst the latter, are quite a number of clubs, such as Otley of National One, that take a very pragmatic view of their situation, desiring to avoid both promotion and relegation; both options being financially impossible for them to deal with. And yet it is those clubs that remain the main public face of the game in the smaller towns across England.

Among the National League's members can be found a number of clubs, like the Bedford Blues, which have successfully managed to use it as a refuge while they recovered from the financial after shock of a spell in the Premiership. Others have been less fortunate. The cost of aiming high has been very high in some cases, as two of the RFU's oldest members found to their cost. Both London Scottish and Richmond were driven into administration and their professional operations merged in with London Irish. For a while, it appeared that both clubs would disband, but they rallied and re-appeared as amateur outfits. Having regained the use of the Richmond Athletic Ground and coped with the shock of being demoted eight divisions, the pair have worked their way back to the top of the regional league structure. Whether the members of either of them, after their painful experiences, still aspire to rejoin the Premiership is open to question.

It has been at times a turbulent passage, but professional club rugby union appears at last to have settled into a good working relationship with the RFU. Currently, the major changes such as franchising the membership of the Premiership and ending promotion and relegation or introducing central contracts are on hold and while they stay that way the relationship will probably remain amicable. Change is certainly not ruled out and the Premiership keeps reviewing new opportunities, such as the early season Anglo-Welsh competition, if it believes they will prove to be lucrative. As it continues to exploit the financial strength it already possesses, the Guinness Premiership is likely to become an even more dominant force in the future life of English Rugby Union.

6. Days of hope... and glory

In the not too distant future, September 2007 to be precise, rugby league will complete its first century of international competition. Over those 100 years the path of international rugby league has not always been a smooth one. At times it has stood accused, quite rightly, of being too predictable and too narrow. At others it has produced some of the most magnificent contests the game has known. As it approaches its centenary, international rugby league should be enjoying its maturity, but instead in its later years it has been beset by periodic crises that have on occasion thrown into question its very existence.

International fixtures were a late addition to the programme of rugby league, as the isolation imposed by the decision to split from the RFU blocked them for the first 12 years of its existence. However, that did not stop the rebels eagerly seizing the opportunity to meet another nation on the field of play when it presented itself. That opportunity came in the form of the 'professional All Blacks' who arrived in England in the autumn of 1907. Three months of club matches helped the tourists get acquainted with the laws of the new game, before facing up to their first internationals. The honour of being the New Zealanders' first national opponents fell to the Welsh, who beat them at Aberdare on New Year's Day 1908. Two weeks later they met England at Wigan. Just before the end of the month they met the first ever team to represent the whole of the Northern Union in the first ever test match at Headingley.

The extra dimension provided by international competition fired the public's imagination, enthused the players and brought the game invaluable publicity and revenue. The Kangaroos made their debut the following year and rapidly established themselves as the team to beat. International and test football had arrived and over the next few years ingrained itself into the fabric of the game as its highest and most prestigious level. Then just before the outbreak of the Second World War the French were welcomed into that select band. Around their contests a whole raft of epic tales, legends and expectations was woven in each of the four countries.

For nearly all of the first 60 years the British Lion was ranked number one with the Kangaroo a close second. However, at the end of the 1960s the Northern Rugby League engine that had powered Great Britain to the top began to falter. As the League's playing standards stagnated and even slipped, it struggled to supply sufficient test class players to keep the British team on top. As Britain's strength ebbed, the Sydney Premiership was only too willing and able to don the mantle of the world's strongest club competition. Becoming the league world's centre of excellence meant that Sydney was able to turn out a steady flow of high quality players, who would in turn become the mainstays of Australia's future run of success.

To suffer a whitewash in one Ashes series was bad enough, but it looked likely that Australia would inflict this ignominy on the Lions for a fifth consecutive time. Only a totally unexpected performance by Great Britain prevented this in the third test in July 1988. During this dismal sequence, Great Britain even found it hard to get the better of the Kiwis. As Australian crowds would not pay in sufficient numbers to watch matches involving a feeble French team their tours down under were cancelled. Europe's declining playing standards pushed the old international order, based on regular tours and world cups, to the point of financial collapse.

A change for the better could be detected in the 1990s as the Great Britain team managed to take each Ashes series to a deciding third test. Further good news came in 1992. The World Cup was then run as a league competition, using the results of a series of designated matches spread over the previous three years, which determined the top two countries to contest a Final. Australia qualified to meet Great Britain at Wembley in October 1992 where a world record international match crowd of 73,631 saw the Kangaroos gain a narrow 10-6 win. It had taken well over 20 years, but there appeared reasonable grounds to believe that Great Britain was on its way back to the top.

On that rising tide of optimism, the Rugby Football League's (RFL) leadership laid plans for its centenary celebrations. For the Centenary's centrepiece, the RFL decided to promote a World Cup tournament, the first for 18 years. Twelve months later, all the planning for that tournament was suddenly thrown into jeopardy when Rupert Murdoch launched his attempt to grab the television rights to Australian Rugby League. Needing the money, the RFL and the New Zealand Rugby League (NZRL) threw in their lot with Murdoch's Newscorp at the start of April 1995. Despite finding itself on the opposite side to the RFL as the battle with Newscorp worked its way through the Australian courts, the ARL remained committed to entering the tournament. That level of co-operation was not maintained with those players who had signed on for Murdoch's competitor League – they were excluded from the teams picked to meet the Kiwis and later the World Cup party.

1995 World Cup

The 11th World Cup, held in October 1995, was the game's biggest- ever international gathering and briefly dispelled the gloomy news emanating from Australia. An unprecedented 10 countries were brought together in the main event and a further seven entered an Emerging Nations competition that ran alongside the main tournament. Hopes that Great Britain would continue its international recovery were dashed when it was agreed that England and Wales would enter the tournament separately. Besides those two there were four existing test playing countries – Australia, France, New Zealand and Papua New Guinea – and four newcomers to the international arena – Fiji, Tonga, South Africa and Western Samoa.

A game that had been stigmatised for years as staid and unadventurous suddenly bristled with exotic newcomers. And those newcomers had not just come to make up the numbers. Tonga were a revelation in Group two, thrilling the fans as they threatened to pull off not one, but two upsets. Cheered on by the locals the Tongans put up a huge performance at Warrington that was only denied by a last minute Kiwi drop-goal. In their next match at Hull the Tongans once again delighted the locals by leading for most of the match before a more experienced Papua New Guinea forced a late draw. The Group three decider was held at Swansea, where a capacity crowd cheered home a Welsh team that displayed bags of courage and quite a bit of skill to overcome an extremely physical Samoan challenge. None of them made it through to the final stages where Australia and New Zealand played out an epic semi-final at Huddersfield that was only decided in extra-time. Although it eventually had a predictable outcome, an Australian victory, the event was acclaimed a major success. Solid support in the Rugby League heartlands allied to higher than expected attendances at Wembley and in South Wales, meant the tournament generated good profits.

Even the absence of those players who had signed for Newscorp had not diminished the Kangaroos' standing in anyway. Such was the depth of talent in Australia that the Kangaroos seemed able to find more than adequate replacements without too much trouble. In fact, the Kangaroos retention of a title they had held for 20 years only served to confirm Australian claims that they could field three or four Test teams, all of them capable of defeating a British team.

Most of the positive aspects of the tournament were lost as the severe problems facing the divided international game once more took centre stage. The old Rugby League International Board had been rendered inoperable by the Australian schism. As Newscorp held the allegiance of the RFL and the NZRL, the tests scheduled for 1996 between Australia and New Zealand and that year's British tour to Australia had to be cancelled. It was a sad way for the last of the old style Lions off season tours to pass into history. Instead the Lions had to content themselves with visiting New Zealand, Papua New Guinea and the South Pacific in October.

That was the first tour to be undertaken after the formation of Super League and the switch to summer and it highlighted the problems touring would now face; tours would be truncated affairs and would have to be confined to a slot after the Australian and British domestic seasons had ended. For nearly 80 years rugby league fans in both hemispheres had regarded the old style winter tours as the pinnacle of international football and they had to be convinced that in their new truncated form there was no loss of commitment or tradition.

Abandoned by its old partners, the ARL was left isolated and could only look on in horror when it appeared that the old International Board would be supplanted by a hastily convened Super League International Board. Fortunately, the uncertainty and bitterness were checked when, in December 1997, the game in Australia decided to reunify and that paved the way for the various international factions to be reconciled. Unfortunately, that coming together crowded the Australian season and brought about the demise of the ARL's main contribution to international development, the annual World Sevens. In August 1998, a new body, the Rugby League International Federation (RLIF), was established and charged with re-establishing an international programme. By the end of the year, a Tri-Nations Tournament, to be held in Australasia in 1999, and a World Cup, to be held in Europe in 2000, had been announced.

The schism in Australia had if anything increased that country's disenchantment with the international game. As far as the sceptics were concerned the annual the Trans-Tasman Tests were all the international football a country needed if it already had the best club competition, the Australian National Rugby League (NRL), and the State of Origin series. In a bid to re-launch international rugby league down under, the re-named Great Britain and Ireland Lions were invited to take part in a Tri-Nations tournament in October 1999. Initially it was intended to host the tournament in both Australia and New Zealand, but in the end Australia's lack of interest meant Auckland staged three of the tournament's four matches. The only match that Australia was interested in hosting was the meeting of the Lions and the Kangaroos. Having already struggled in a warm up match against a Gold Coast junior team, public interest in Brisbane was so low that the match drew a record low crowd of only 12,944. The few that turned out saw the Lions slump to a record defeat on Australian soil. It was an outcome that according to many Australian commentators effectively put the block on international football for the foreseeable future.

Not surprisingly, it took nearly three years before the RLIF attempted once more to revive Australian interest in the international game. At its March 2002 meeting the RLIF decided that every July Great Britain would play a one-off test in Australasia – in Australia in 2002, in New Zealand the following year and so on. Hoping to build on their improved showing at home in the previous year's Ashes series, the Lions returned to Sydney after an interval of 10 years. Still suffering from jet lag the British team were thrown straight in against a Kangaroo team that was still fired up from the recently completed State of Origin series. With the odds stacked against them the Lions did try to make a fight of it in front of a reasonable crowd, but a second-half collapse led to a humiliating new record defeat. Great Britain's stock in Sydney had once more hit rock bottom. Whether the score-line was a true reflection of the play or not, as some claimed, the result was another huge setback for the international game in Australia. The only good thing to come from the match was the recognition on the RLIF's part that Australia was just too far away from Europe to play one-off test matches.

Nothing that has happened since then has convinced the Australians that their scepticism about the international game is in anyway misplaced and that is the main issue the RLIF has to tackle. There is a crucial role that the RFL can play to assist the RLIF for it appears that only a successful British or English team will be able to revitalise the prospects for the international game in Australia. If a winning British team is the short-term key to the whole international situation, how can the Lions escape the 'nearly men' tag and become successful? Australian commentators put forward various schemes in an attempt to offer assistance. One scheme envisaged talented British players being assigned to NRL clubs to help them sharpen their skills. Rather than have the players spread across the NRL, another suggestion had the Great Britain test team operating as a separate club in the NRL. These schemes were never practical, but in the absence of any Australian enthusiasm, international football became something that took place in Europe.

During November 2000 the RFL upstaged the 1995 event by staging an even bigger combined World Cup tournament and an Emerging Nations competition. Determined to make the World Cup a European event, one group was hosted in France, one in Ireland and Scotland and one in Wales and the west of England. In addition, the tournament used venues in the game's traditional northern heartland. Also used for the first time were rugby union stadiums as Kingsholm, Stradey Park and Twickenham. As previously agreed by the RLIF, Great Britain was once again replaced by teams from the four home nations. Unfortunately, due to the return of most converts to rugby union, the Irish, Scottish and Welsh squads were less well-known in the countries they represented, being heavily dependent on players who qualified through the birthplace of their parents or grandparents. Instead of the original planned 12, 16 nations entered – Australia, Cook Islands, England, Fiji, France, Ireland, Lebanon, Maoris, New Zealand, Papua New Guinea, Russia, Scotland, South Africa, Tonga, Wales and Western Samoa.

While the tournament organisers were guilty of over-extending the event behind the scenes, on the field it was certainly providing some wonderful occasions, culminating in a superb Final between Australia and New Zealand at Old Trafford. Over the four weeks, braving lots of atrociously wet, cold weather, that nearly caused the postponement of several matches and severely dislocated the transport system, almost 250,000 watched the tournament. When the tournament ended, the organisers were still predicting a profit of £1,000,000, but mistakes had been made and expenditure had run out of control. Months later it had to be admitted that rather than deliver the anticipated profit, the competition would return losses approaching £2,000,000. Much of the anticipated profit had been earmarked for a number of the game's international development projects and many were suddenly left high and dry.

It was the worst possible outcome in all ways. Confidence was damaged, losses had to be recouped and crucially, in England, it allowed the main club owners to reopen the old club versus country debate. Instead of capitalising on the World Cup's limited successes, the club owners moved to block any expansion of international football. Chris Caisley, the chairman of Super League Europe, responding in December 2000 to proposals for a home international series, stated negatively that "... people have to accept that the strength of our competition lies in our club game". It was a short-sighted view that come back to haunt the English game later that year. When the rugby union recruiters came calling that summer, nearly all those who succumbed, such as Iestyn Harris and Henry Paul, stressed the importance that the increased opportunity to play in big international events had played in their decision. When the RLIF reassembled in March 2002, it laid down a three-year schedule of matches. Each season in the northern hemisphere would start with the World Club Challenge. For the southern hemisphere opener, the World Sevens was restarted and would as before help provide a focus for the emerging nations. The meeting also agreed that the Kiwis and the Kangaroos would visit Europe in 2002 and 2003 respectively. This was a welcome and safe schedule which was secured by the knowledge that British crowds, undeterred by the form book, would continue to turn out and make tests involving either the Kangaroos or the Kiwis financially viable. Without the enthusiasm of the fans in Britain, it is doubtful whether tours, world cups and latterly the Tri-Nations could have been kept alive.

New initiatives

Richard Lewis was appointed as the RFL's new executive chairman in March 2002 and after having had the chance to review the situation he remarked the following August that "the sports that are doing well are those who have got their act together on the international front". Rugby league was most certainly not one of those. Lewis started work to change that and in January 2003 was prominent in the launch of a new European Rugby League Federation. The British and French Leagues also established three new regional international tournaments – the European Nations Cup, the Mediterranean Cup and the Victory Cup in Russia – to put European expansion on a more organised footing. In the light of experience, the RLIF revised its international programme in March 2003. Great Britain's one-off tests were removed and the proposed 2005 World

Cup postponed. In their place came a new Tri-Nations tournament, to be held in Britain, which would run annually for three years from autumn 2004. While that programme did not provide regular international competition for all members, it did have the advantage of focusing on the game's immediate strengths.

While the RLIF was searching for a successful fixture formula, their old adversary was demonstrating just how bountiful international football could be. By any reckoning 2003 was a remarkable year for English rugby union. After a slow start, the year built up to a veritable explosion of media adulation as the English team returned in triumph from Australia with the William Webb Ellis trophy. It had been a truly remarkable World Cup Final; England winning with the last kick of extra-time to silence the bellicose Wallabies in their own backyard. English sporting pride had apparently been restored and all the memories of recent setbacks and disappointments that other sports had suffered on an international level were swept away. Almost overnight, rugby union had restored the feel good factor to English sport.

Comparisons with the World Cup triumph of 1966 were perhaps a little bit wide of the mark, but they were close enough to provide a basis for the media to have a go at soccer, which coincidentally was going through one of its periodic crises. Suddenly the highly paid stars of the Barclaycard Premiership were being attacked in the media as ungrateful, soft, spoilt brats who did not deserve the affections of the nation. Unexpectedly, there was a vacancy for a more 'wholesome' alternative.

In its turn, the media 'discovered' professional rugby union, turning the England team into national heroes and its main playmaker, the intensely professional Jonny Wilkinson, into a household name. In return for the headlines and the features, the media granted rugby union a period of grace in which not only could it do no wrong, but it would also be heaped with praises for all the positive virtues it embodied. It was clear in the run up firstly to the BBC's Sports Personality of the Year Awards and then the New Year's Honours List that the media would orchestrate a campaign to ensure that the rugby union squad would be well rewarded.

Certainly something new had happened for during the six weeks of rising hopes and emotions that constituted the World Cup finals the English public had connected with rugby union in an unprecedented way. For once it was not the national football team setting record television viewing figures or pulling an amazing threequarters of a million people onto London's streets to welcome them home. Thanks to the power of television, old prejudices were broken down and an audience far beyond the boundaries of rugby union's traditional support was tapped.

There was no need to wait to gain further access to that new audience for the annual Six Nations tournament followed hot on the heels of the World Cup. Recently concentrated into a seven-week format, the old tournament was the perfect vehicle to focus the attention of the game's supporters and the media through to the spring. The legendary old tournament had been a fixture on the nation's sporting calendar for years and its modernisation was an object lesson in how to mould older tradition's to fit contemporary professional needs. While England's quest for the Grand Slam may have failed, the tournament excelled itself as usual, with nearly every match sold-out and television audiences up yet again.

Nearly all the commentators in the media saw the World Cup victory as opening up unprecedented opportunities for rugby union in England. Just parading the World Cup trophy around Zurich Premiership grounds would cause sold-out signs to be posted, in some cases for the first time. By harnessing the positive effect of the successes of the national team's victory, there appeared to be a good chance that the decline in playing numbers at both club and school level, which had become a cause for concern since the advent of professionalism, could be halted and even reversed. Even more significantly, it appeared to offer a real prospect for union to make a great leap forward and expand its playing base beyond the affluent suburbs.

All those benefits were showered on rugby union thanks to a well promoted and regular international programme. Naturally, anyone involved with rugby league would want their game to enjoy the same sort of benefits. Some actually did come league's way for the public often failed to differentiate between the two games and lent their support to the most prominent local club regardless. To go beyond that the RLIF needs to become stronger, receive a greater commitment from its leading members and vigorously promote a regular international programme. If that strengthening does not take place then all that those involved with league can do is envy the good fortune of their union counterparts.

Without doubt, a successful national team would work wonders for league's profile in Britain. A successful team would also provide a vehicle for leading individuals to transcend their club environment and build their own national profile. In today's sporting world, a well promoted national team is indispensable to attract the attention of sponsors and the media and to create the working partnerships capable of generating the kind of income that can fund many future development programmes.

For league's international programme to become a real success, the seemingly permanent aura of Kangaroo invincibility must be placed under serious threat. Any ideas that the Australians' aura will suddenly become less than invincible because they will sit back and rest on their laurels are well wide of the mark. Only if the challengers raise their own national standards can the Kangaroos be toppled. Various coaches have chased unsuccessfully the dream of a successful British team for nearly 40 years and know from experience that their skills alone cannot raise the team above constraints that are inherent within the British game.

Even though the Australians have the strongest club competition in the world, the NRL, the State of Origin series still occupies a prime position in their domestic calendar. Over the years the Australians have reaped untold benefits from having the Origin series as an intermediate stage for players seeking to ready themselves for the higher demands of test football. At one time the County Championship provided the British game with the kind of representative matches that most closely approximate to the annual Australian State of Origin series. That had stopped being the case long before the RFL abolished the County Championship in 1982 and subsequent attempts to create a meaningful equivalent based on Lancashire meeting Yorkshire, marketed either as 'The War of the Roses' or 'The County of Origin', have failed. Not even declaring that match a test trial managed to dispel an obvious lack of commitment at all levels that blighted and undermined the event. While the old northern counties seem too parochial to excite much future interest, the game has not yet spread far enough for a future north versus south match to be viable.

With meaningful representative matches proving difficult to sustain, the entire responsibility for ensuring that Britain's leading players and coaches developed the individual and team skills necessary to match the best that the Kangaroos could muster fell on Super League's clubs. By raising competitiveness to NRL levels Super League would supposedly bring this about. According to this scenario, the players in Super League would have to face the similar week-in, week-out intensity as their Australian counterparts and that would prepare a Great Britain team to meet Australia on at least equal terms.

Getting clubs and country to share the same interests is never that easy. Where Super League clubs want ready made players who can deliver immediate results, the national team needs a longer term plan for player development. To make up for the shortfall of home grown Test class players, far too many of Super League's leading clubs have been only too willing to fill their teams with often veteran overseas players; a short sighted policy that was only partially successful even in domestic terms. This tendency has at times been particularly detrimental in driving British players out of the key decision making positions.

It has taken time, but arguably the vast majority of the individual members of the British test team are now on a par with their opposite numbers in the green and gold. Yet, when it comes to playing pressure football, a gulf can still become apparent. Having grown used to playing under pressure in very competitive matches, the Kangaroos have always managed to raise their game when it was needed, whereas Great Britain have never had the mental toughness to match them. It is now not so much a question of individual ability or the ability of the British team to follow a game plan, but their ability, both individually and collectively to apply and absorb pressure at the highest level.

Weaknesses as glaring as that may soon be a thing of the past as youth development, which has been one of the success stories of Super League years, may have been laying the foundations that will make a decisive contribution to the international game. Academies have been in operation at many British clubs and they have for many years been producing a steady stream of well-coached young players. It was recognised that something more needed to be done for those players, who had the potential to move beyond club level. Although David Waite is best remembered for his work as head coach, it is arguable that his greatest contribution to British rugby league was through his other job as performance director. In the latter role, he played a crucial role in creating a development structure for league's elite performers. Under Waite's direction, time and money was invested to build up a strong England under-18 Academy team. When in December 2002, the Australian Combined High Schools, visited Britain, the Academy team was ready and surprised many by beating them twice. As if to prove this was no fluke, the Academy team beat them again, this time down under in August 2004. By then, there were promising signs that the Academy's products were making their mark at Super League and even test level.

After some difficult years, there was a really positive atmosphere around international rugby league in 2004 – once the intended year for the 13th World Cup. The Tri-Nations series involving Australia, Great Britain and New Zealand got underway in Auckland in mid-October before transferring to Britain one week later. The tournament proved a big success in Britain, its six matches drawing big crowds and generating lots of good publicity and receipts. Predictably the tournament Final ended in another cruel disappointment for Great Britain at the hands of the Kangaroos. Although the Lions had got the better of the Australians in one group match, the Final showed that the men from down under were still way ahead and on their best form still virtually unbeatable. One of the spin-off benefits of having the Kangaroos and the Kiwis over in Europe for five weeks was that it provided a chance for France to take them on, on free weekends, in 'friendly' internationals.

Ever since the switch to summer, Great Britain's international preparation and test matches have been confined to a few weeks at the end of each domestic season. Britain's opposition in those tests has been provided by either the Kangaroos or the Kiwis. Tests against the most obvious and closest opponent, France, used to be a regular feature, but were removed from Great Britain's fixture list in 1994-95 to allow England and Wales to get some match practice prior to the Centenary World Cup. Since then, only a pre-Ashes warm-up test in late October 2001 had been arranged. Reacting to several heavy French defeats during that time, many within the RFL concluded that France was too weak to play test matches, and that they should look for fixtures with lesser opponents.

It has taken time, but France may well have confounded those gloomy predictions and be on the verge of becoming a test class opponent once more. Good performances in those matches against Australia and New Zealand in 2004 seem to indicate that France might be on the way to overcoming its tactical shortcomings, especially on defence and its lack of adequate technical coaching and physical preparation that have undermined the team's standing for years. There was further good news, this time at youth level, where the French League retains an extensive network and was capable of fielding an under-18 Academy team that could hold their peers at Hull FC to a draw and succumb to defeat only by one and two points respectively at St Helens and Leeds in February 2005.

Three months later, Great Britain's management, looking for more international opportunities suggested that a mid-season test against France might resume in 2006, provided Super League could make a free weekend available. There was even more good news. According to the latest RLIF schedule, France should make a tour down under in 2007.

There is so much to look forward to, but as always with League's international programme the future is always spiced up with a little bit of uncertainty and doubt. Not even the success of the 2004 Tri-Nations could make a rerun of the tournament the following year a certainty. Australian concerns about player burnout almost scuppered the next competition until some changes to the format allayed them. Thankfully everything had been sorted out in time for those attending the RLIF meeting in March 2005 to agree that the Tri-Nations will be staged in Britain once more in the autumn of 2005.

After that, the RLIF has laid on a programme that should excite every British League fan. After an absence of seven years, the RLIF has decided that it's time for a Great Britain team to appear for a series of matches down under once more. To do this it has re-located the 2006 Tri-Nations series to Australasia. On the evidence of past tours, there ought to be a large contingent of fans following that British team down under. Hopefully, those travelling fans and the international game will both get what they deserve, a British team that can beat the Kangaroos.

Not long after the British team gets back from its trip, it will be time for the RFL to lay on the celebrations at home. The Great Britain team will hopefully serve up a real festival of rugby league for their fans in November 2007, when the Kiwis will visit to mark the centenary of their pioneering tour. When the Kiwis leave the Great Britain team will go into hibernation, for how long is not clear, while the Home nations once more take their place on the world stage. A World Cup tournament, to celebrate the centenary of the New South Wales RFL, is scheduled for 2008. It is to be hoped that this World Cup tournament marks the start of a new, regular four yearly cycle that enables the competition to really become the international heartbeat of the game.

95

Rugby union Zurich Premiership action: Steve Sooialo passing for Harlequins against Leeds Tykes. (Photo: David Williams)

Former Bradford Bulls rugby league star Tevita Vaikona playing rugby union for Saracens. (Photo: David Williams)

7. Shock; horror; rugby league extinct... yet again.

I have long held the view that there is one characteristic more than anything else which identifies the genuine, dyed-in-the-wool rugby league supporter – a deeply held, almost innate sense of grievance.

It's a general, non-specific grievance beyond the obvious – referees, touch judges and those charged with running the game both at club level and the higher echelons. But it is a grievance which at its strongest and most developed draws from an entrenched generalised resentment, rooted in a mix of class consciousness, caste, nationalism and, most importantly, long and bitter experience.

It manifests itself in the deep suspicion with which those from outside what, in rather dated terms, are described as the 'heartland' areas of the game are viewed. It is the product of generations perceiving themselves to have been done down and deceived by outsiders, especially those falling into the category of rugby union types from the south of England.

Ten years on from the historic events of 1995 – in particular the acceptance of open professionalism by rugby union – it is interesting to reflect on why this commonly held characteristic still remains prevalent, marring, some would say, the relationship between the two codes which in many other respects has never been better.

I was reminded of this recurring theme by the remarks of Clare Balding, the BBC sports presenter, when she addressed this year's annual dinner of the Parliamentary Rugby League Group. Having spoken at length of her admiration and passion for rugby league, she focussed critically on what she termed the "chippiness" of many of its followers. The persecution complex of so many in the game was, in her view, its major negative – an outdated, unjustified attitude that detracted from the overwhelmingly positive picture of a modern, vibrant sport. It was time, she implied, for rugby league people to grow up, celebrate and be proud of what they had.

Now, I have had a lifetime's experience of trying to explain to 'outsiders' why we rugby league people have had every reason to be "chippy" from as far back as the developments fostering the idea of a Northern Union some time before 1895. One hundred and ten years later (and a decade on from the establishment of free movement between the codes) it is a simple fact of life that I, and many thousands of others who care passionately about the sport, feel as aggrieved as ever about the way rugby league seems deliberately done down on a range of fronts. After what I genuinely believe has been a decade of progress for the sport on-and-off the field, why do I and so many others have – in Clare Balding's terms – chips on our shoulders which are bigger than ever?

Over the past 10 years it has been fascinating to follow the comparative development of both union and league in new eras for both sports. There have been striking parallels in some of the issues faced – the debate around promotion and relegation, for example, reflecting broadly the same arguments within the separate codes. Both have made progress in respect of the quality of what is on offer on the field of play, with full-time professionalism paying obvious dividends in relation to player fitness and skill levels. Both have seen – at club level in the Zurich Premiership and the Engage Super League – a significant growth in spectator attendances. While union has continued its longstanding supremacy on the international front, with the 2003 World Cup victory proving a huge selling point for the code, league's Tri-Nations formula appears to have the potential to deliver a long-overdue resurrection of serious international competition. And, as evidenced for example by the joint training initiative this year at Headingley involving Leeds Rhinos RLFC and the England rugby union team, there now appears to be greater than ever mutual respect at management, coaching and playing levels in each code.

Against this background it is therefore all the more difficult to explain the reasons why the media treatment of both games over the past decade has been so markedly different. While union has gained increasing column inches, including in some newspapers which, until recently, rarely mentioned the sport, league's national media coverage is at best miserly and at worst frequently non-existent. And when league does gain some detailed attention it is noticeable that such coverage is more often than not either negative or openly hostile.

Our own public service broadcaster – the BBC – has, in my opinion, for a long time led the field in terms of an almost abject disregard for rugby league at national level, while at the same time projecting and promoting union in sometimes unjustifiable and indefensible ways. This marked difference in the treatment of the two codes by the BBC is nothing new. Long before the Corporation had the excuse of league 'selling out' to BSkyB, its incredible choice of the England rugby union team as "Team of the Year" in the 1993 *BBC Sports Personality of the Year* awards left even Twickenham almost speechless. Bearing in mind that England had won neither the Grand Slam or what was then the Five Nations Championship, even Dudley Wood, the secretary of the RFU, was forced to concede that the justification for the award "was tenuous to say the least and ....came as something of an embarrassment to us." (Letter 13 January 1994 from Dudley Wood to Mr. J. Brownlow of Bolton).

In that same year, the Great Britain rugby league team had achieved the first home series whitewash against New Zealand in 20 years and Wigan RLFC had just won a fifth successive Championship and Challenge Cup double. Away from the oval ball, the England Women's cricket team had won the World Championship, Manchester United had been the first winners of the FA Premier League and the British athletics team had produced some brilliant performances in difficult circumstances in the World Championships in Stuttgart.

The suspicions of many rugby league followers that, in marked contrast to its attitude to union, there was a scarcely hidden BBC agenda of outright hostility to their sport was confirmed in particular by the manner in which BBC Radio Five chose to cover the opening of the 2000 Super League season. Its *On The Line* programme (2 March 2000) focussed on the claims of a Sheffield University student that the game was in serious decline.

Regardless of the fact that her analysis of the sport was narrow, her conclusions controversial and open to considerable challenge, they were carried as almost indisputable fact in several prominent newspaper reports linked to the BBC programme. The fact that several publications headlined the content of the BBC programme on the morning before it was broadcast indicated that – most unusually for the BBC – the Corporation had taken considerable trouble to promote this particular rugby league feature.

The consequences included a two page article in the *Daily Express* headed "Investigation reveals a game in crisis." The *Daily Mirror* coverage, describing the student's claims as "an explosive *BBC* report" (my emphasis), was headlined "Is Rugby League a dying game?" Their article talked of the game having "plummeting gates" when the BBC programme actually conceded that attendances had in fact increased. The reference to "Wigan *Wanderers*" in *Mirror* editor Piers Morgan's subsequent defence of the article didn't exactly inspire confidence in his paper's command of what was happening in the sport. (Letter dated 6 June 2000 from *Daily Mirror* to Press Complaints Commission)

I discovered from a subsequent conversation with a rugby league journalist on one of the papers which had covered the BBC programme that the content of the article he had filed - which had contradicted their key conclusions - had been altered to portray an almost wholly negative picture of the sport. A more positive piece by someone in contact with the game on a daily basis in the north of England had been altered to suit the London editorial line of rugby league being in terminal decline.

It is hard to avoid the conclusion that the BBC deliberately chose to trumpet a particularly negative angle on Super League in part, at least, in response to rugby league's deal with BSkyB. I have several items of correspondence from BBC sources which implies that, as league 'sold out' to Murdoch, it must live with the consequences in terms of the Corporation's approach to the sport.

Media sources feed on each other and the thoughts of a single university student lead to a widespread wholly negative portrayal of the game at a time when any objective analysis of the sport as a whole would have seen some very positive pointers for the future at both the professional and amateur level.

The Rugby League World Cup, held in appalling weather in the autumn of 2000, was widely perceived as the nadir of the Super League era and, although they didn't exactly need it, gave the sport's knockers in the national media a new focus for negativity. The BBC – with broadcasting rights to the competition – did some half-hearted promotion for its coverage but the competition never recovered from dismal images of the rain-soaked, half-deserted stadia of the opening matches. A British crowd of some 44,000 at Old Trafford for a final between Australia and New Zealand would, in the past have been regarded as remarkable success. But the lasting impression of the 2000 World Cup was of an over-ambitious, badly organised competition which landed the Rugby Football League with huge financial debts.

The months following the World Cup saw sections of the London media all but declare open season on the sport of rugby league. League had been "thrown to the Lions" according to a full page *Sunday Express* article by the paper's chief sport correspondent, Jim Holden, which appeared on the morning after supporters of the XIII-a-side game had packed Twickenham for the 2001 Challenge Cup Final. Focusing on Jason Robinson's switch to union, he even threw in the infamous quote of 1930 rugby union Lions tour manager, James Baxter, about rugby league being a sport of the "sewers".

To their credit, in the following week's edition, his paper published two full pages of letters strongly refuting his argument that union's acquisition of league players meant that it had won the power battle of the codes. Correspondents argued that no other sport, after attracting 68,000 people to any of its matches, would have to suffer the attacks that rugby league had come to expect from a union-dominated national press. In no other branch of sports journalism did there appear to be as much "vitriol" as there seemed to be towards rugby league. (*Sunday Express* 6 May 2001)

"Great game, rugby league, such a shame it has to die" headlined Frank Keating's article in *The Guardian* on the following day. In all seriousness he suggested that league would be gone by 2006. "To my mind" he wrote "these last few months have seen rugby league totally doomed. It is only a matter of time – and not much of that either – before rugby league in Britain is forced to merge with a voracious union. I give it five years and that is being generous."

Again on the back of Robinson's move to union he asked how many former league men will be union Lions when they next toured in 2005. "Plenty", was his answer and there would be "even more" who had played in the 2000 Rugby League World Cup and would enjoy their next world cup as union players in 2003.

It was Keating's belief that "low key, dismal unwatched World Cups on the back of mundane club contests against the same blokes you played

100

against a fortnight ago and three weeks before that, and for local reporters in northern editions, are no use any more for top sportsmen desperate for the incentive of genuine glory." Union could deliver it and league could not. (*The Guardian* 7 May 2001)

Played at the same venue as league's 2000 World Cup Final, the concept of a Super League Grand Final has, in contrast to the last World Cup, emerged as one of the great successes of the game since the changes introduced in 1995. Crowds at the Grand Final have gradually increased until sell outs at Old Trafford have become the norm. Nevertheless, *The Times* sports columnist, Simon Barnes, chose the occasion of the 2001 match to suggest that rugby league was on the verge of extinction. With Henry Paul playing his last game for Bradford in the Final before joining Gloucester rugby union club, his article suggested that "league as a financially viable sport was dying on its feet in 2001." (*The Times* 13 October 2001)

Barnes' piece – obviously written before the completion of the match report which appeared alongside it – made no mention of the fact that the Final had attracted a record attendance of over 60,000 spectators. It made no mention of spectator attendances at club games or reference to the remarkable expansion of amateur rugby league outside its northern strongholds through the game's summer Rugby League Conference.

It was yet another piece of deliberate negativity about the game fed into the national psyche. It was one more contribution to a perception of a game that leads senior journalists of the likes of Colin Gibson, Sports Editor of the *Daily Mail*, to describe rugby league as "a sport which has an ever diminishing support base." (Letter to author 18 December 2001)

While not necessarily subscribing to the totality of the theory that all British news originates from a media loop located in certain London wine bars, I have no doubt whatsoever that once a notion becomes established in the capital's media circles it becomes very difficult to contradict. Sporting soothsayers such as Holden, Keating, Barnes and company may have little contemporary experience of what is happening in the world of rugby league but their thoughts are widely communicated and influence significantly the attitudes of many others in the London based media and corporate sector in respect of their outlook towards the game.

Such people rely for their understanding of rugby league on an extremely narrow menu of markers which feature no real knowledge of the code beyond the existence of a handful of top players – who have usually at some point been speculatively linked with union – and three or four Super League clubs. Their command of the subject is based on a perception of international competition being the be-all and end-all of sport. They appear ignorant of the fact that some of the most successful sports in the world – American Football and Aussie Rules being just two examples – have no real international element at all. They simply do not understand that significant numbers in rugby league would actually

101

enthuse more over a Featherstone versus Castleford National League One match than Great Britain versus Australia. They miss completely the essence and strength of rugby league – the fact that it is still very largely and very proudly a community based sport.

This is precisely why generations of harbingers of doom in the London media – I have been reading their dire predictions all my adult life – continue to make fools of themselves forecasting its imminent demise. They have never understood that, beyond their superficial view of the code, are extensive rugby league communities whose roots are a good deal stronger than those of many other sports.

I recall being particularly struck by the ease with which, after a century in existence, producing county players and internationals and competing at the very top of the sport, Wakefield Rugby Union Club slipped quietly out of existence a couple of years ago, almost unnoticed. There were barely any protests and only minimal publicity. What a contrast to the public outrage expressed in the same community a few years earlier when it was proposed that Wakefield Trinity RLFC should merge with Featherstone Rovers and Castleford.

The difference is that rugby league has a bit more to it than the superficial features which afford key figures in the London media such a limited grasp of the game. But we shouldn't be surprised at the extent of their ignorance. When the political battle over free movement between the codes was at its fiercest in the early 1990s, I recall being astonished that numerous London-based political correspondents had absolutely no idea that the vast majority of rugby league was played by amateurs. Most believed the code was wholly professional, just as most of their colleagues contributing even now to the sporting pages haven't the least idea of the extent of the amateur game and its expansion throughout many areas of Great Britain.

Perhaps we should take some comfort from the fact that, by and large, Andy Farrell's departure to rugby union has not so far generated the usual predictions of rugby league extinction. Perhaps the prospect of a 29-year-old rugby league prop, whose knees have required considerable medical attention in recent seasons, appearing as seriously proposed at centre or stand-off for the England rugby union team, was just too sharp a reflection of the relative on-field merits of the two codes. Perhaps - although they don't say it - some of our sports commentators appreciate that ageing rugby league players can significantly extend their playing careers by moving across to what some of them clearly regard as the considerably less demanding on-field environment of XV-a-side.

But let's not forget that allied to reduced physical demands the attraction of rugby union does often include the guarantee of much greater media attention for the individual player. Linked to the increased opportunity of participation in high profile international competition, their earning potential can be considerably enhanced by consequent product endorsement deals and commercial sponsorship. And if the record of the past five years is anything to go by, it certainly increases the player's chances of being recognised by an honours system which would appear to have as limited an awareness of rugby league as our London based sports writers. (During the 2004 Parliamentary session, an answer to a Parliamentary Question I asked revealed a 53-one union-league honours ratio over the previous five years).

The widely held sense of grievance is therefore an eminently reasonable component of the rugby league enthusiast's make-up. It is, as can be seen, an entirely justifiable endowment within their constitution and arguably their legitimacy could be open to question without it. So if "chippiness" is perceived by some as a flaw in their make-up then these particular critics clearly have some considerable ground to cover in coming to terms with a proper understanding of the sociology of rugby league.

But I admit I have to qualify my defence of 'original grievance' with an appreciation of the fact that rugby league itself has to do a good deal more than it has done so far to regularly and actively challenge the metropolitan templates which are consistently applied, to the detriment of the sport. Far too many within the game shrug their shoulders at such attacks and regard them as inevitable. They are not. They can be effectively challenged, as the totally uncoordinated response to Jim Holden's *Sunday Express* piece showed.

They can firstly be countered by an effective and coordinated approach within the game that recognises its perceived negatives and, where there is legitimate criticism, does something about it. This means taking seriously the widespread belief of many outside rugby league that meaningful international competition is the most effective showcase for any sport. It means understanding that a key by-product of developing the international element should also be the retention of some of the top stars that might otherwise be tempted to cross codes for new challenges and horizons as well as a bigger public profile.

It means listening to those – not all necessarily from outside the game – who, while admiring the speed and spectacle of the contemporary rugby league, believe that the emphasis on impact, power and 'big hits' has come at some cost in terms of a loss of skill. It means thinking through the process of addressing the criticisms of that I, for one, believe just occasionally have some legitimacy. Rugby league's survival and success stems from on-field evolution and innovation and it is time to give serious thought to encouraging the unexpected. Addressing what is regarded by many both within and outside the game as the utter farce of non-competitive scrummaging would be a very useful starting point.

Andy Farrell charging forward for the Great Britain rugby league team.
Now he faces a new challenge playing rugby union.
(Photo: David Williams)

It means, (and as a Yorkshireman it saddens me to say this) taking the reality of the metropolitan power base much more seriously. Richard Lewis, the Rugby Football League's executive chairman, is absolutely right in arguing the need for two London-based Super League clubs in the not-too-distant future. Those in the North who regularly decry 'subsidising' the Broncos in the rugby league press will be aghast at such a proposal, but genuine competition between two top London-based clubs would be a spur to their success and a crucially important component in generating an awareness of the code among metropolitan opinion formers. The Broncos' recent tie-up with Harlequins will undoubtedly be controversial in some quarters, but if it results in an improved profile for London-based rugby league then the implications for the sport as a whole could well be positive.

While it will cost money and was tried in a half-hearted way by Super League Europe some years ago, a London presence beyond just individual clubs is also essential in addressing the game's profile. A 'rapid response' capacity to deal with negative messages about the game should be based there. But rather than just being reactive, it would be the focus for a vigorous strategy of working with media contacts to improve their understanding of the sport. The Rugby Football League have taken steps to commission some work aimed at lifting the media profile which has produced some limited results in terms of improved coverage. Unfortunately, a great deal more is needed if decades of negative coverage and, not infrequently, downright lies about the game are to be countered.

My starting point, for fairly obvious reasons, would be the BBC. As Polly Toynbee put it recently, "The mighty BBC news machine dominates not just in sheer volume, but as a sheet anchor of authority in the rudderless anarchy of what is or isn't 'news'. Other media seize on the agenda chosen by the *Today* programme, *Breakfast* or the *World at One*..." (*The Guardian* 22 June 2005)

But, as I found out in corresponding with the BBC on behalf of the Parliamentary Rugby League Group over a decade and a half, despite being a so-called 'broadcast partner' their corporate attitude to the game gives the distinct impression of, at best, disinterest and, at worst, downright contempt. Our numerous letters to the particular targets of Radio Four's *Today* programme and their weekend news bulletins were precisely because they do indeed in many respects determine the wider news agenda pursued by other media. But the overall impact of our lobbying was usually limited to odd surges in results reporting in the immediate aftermath of representations before a return to non-existence.

Their polite explanations for the absence of any coverage refer the complainant to their Five Live sports coverage or that offered by BBC local radio. Although they don't specifically say it, there is a between the lines message that rugby league people are not expected to be listening to Radio Four. Is the fact that their bulletins regularly cater for those interested in Leeds Tykes' rugby union results but not those of Leeds Rhinos rugby league team determined by their perception of who actually follows each code? Bearing in mind that the Rhinos have an average home gate at least three times that of the Tykes it is clearly not determined by factors relating to the size of the audience. It will be very interesting indeed to compare and contrast their future treatment of the two codes at Harlequins.

The fact that rugby league is seen as of merely 'regional' interest is underlined by the continuing failure to nationally network BBC Two's *Super League Show*. Despite presenter Harry Gration's undoubted professionalism and his personal enthusiasm and commitment to the sport, if one needs any evidence of the BBC's attitude to rugby league it can be seen in its approach to this programme. My definition of a rugby league intellectual is someone who knows when, where and indeed if the *Super League Show* will appear on any particular weekend. The Corporation's attitude to the rugby league supporting viewer appears to be one of complete disregard. Complainants will probably be told about less than encouraging viewing figures, but how on earth is it possible to build up the audience for a programme when people are unclear as to when, or even if, it will appear?

A good example of BBC practice relating to this programme during the most recent rugby league season concerned its scheduling for mid-day on

Sunday 3 July 2005 on BBC One North, North East and North West. Those tuning in found that it had been replaced by the Wimbledon tennis in which any British interest had disappeared some days earlier. It is my understanding that the presenter and interviewees were actually ready to broadcast in the studio when the programme was dropped.

The former BBC *Today* programme presenter Rod Liddle has long argued that the Corporation has consistently been held back by an overwhelmingly middle class agenda and broadcasting workforce. It is unfashionable nowadays to mention the class question but it undoubtedly underpins the BBC's approach to sport in particular. If one uses comparative spectator attendances to evaluate public interest in a sport there can be absolutely no excuse for their treatment of rugby league in comparison to their treatment of tennis, cricket and rugby union. Other factors clearly come into play which are difficult to substantiate but very obvious. League remains – as it always has been – strictly on the outside of the British Establishment.

Some will say we should celebrate such status and be proud of it. But most of those who follow rugby league and want it to progress are rightly dismayed and angered that the game should continue to be held back by the same type of people and attitudes which have dogged it since its formation.

While our print media is in private hands, the BBC operates to a Charter making certain demands of it as a public service broadcaster. The Rugby Football League and the game's followers should take every possible step to establish whether the Corporation is in breach of the spirit of the requirements placed upon it. Their treatment of the sport underpins the attitudes of so many London sports journalists. Getting the BBC to give rugby league fairer, more reasonable and representative treatment has to be the springboard for a belated transformation in the national media coverage of the sport.

So my message – loud and clear – is to move from "chippiness" to challenge. The time to actively counter the negative portrayal of rugby league is long overdue. The media's frequent dismissal and denigration is the final frontier to be conquered in its quest to become established as a major national and international sport. If the game could only unleash and energise that collective sense of grievance and put it too productive use there would be nothing to stop its success.

8. One game good, two games better?

Once the dust had settled, Rupert Murdoch's ground-breaking incursion brought about significant change at the top level of both English rugby games. Super League, fuelled by Murdoch's millions, dragged English rugby league out of its semi-professional lethargy. At the same time the northern members of what was then rugby union's Courage National Leagues were forced to leave the old world of sham-amateurism behind. Both games had to jettison their traditional approaches and focus on new ways of serving up success and entertainment as they pursued a wider audience. It was hardly surprising that two very similar games, both struggling to come to terms with the demands of modern day professionalism, should find ways to feed off each other.

As English rugby union faced up to the possibilities and pitfalls that professionalism presented, it was clear that a new relationship between the two games was starting to evolve. Exactly what shape that relationship would take was dependent on how rugby union evolved. For the leading rugby union clubs in the north, the adoption of professionalism provided them with the opportunity to simultaneously learn from and mount a real challenge to rugby league. In the north-western region some journalists were predicting that two – Orrell and Sale – and possibly three – Liverpool – strong standard bearers capable of competing with their neighbouring Super League clubs, could be established. In making those predictions, those journalists believed that the existing rugby league fan base would be receptive to the appearance of a new form of professional rugby, and would in the right circumstances become a large proportion of union's future swelling crowds.

That expectation, if true, was exactly what the new breed of rugby entrepreneurs wanted to hear. Once they turned professional, both Orrell and Sale's management had to confront two major problems. The first, which was common to both, was how to attract much needed investment. The second was how to build attendances and there Orrell was thought to have an advantage as it would obviously be able to tap into Wigan RLFC's fan base. Sale was thought to be at a slight disadvantage being just outside the rugby league heartland, but someone had a fix for that. When, in July 1996, Frank Warren came calling with the intention of investing in Sale RUFC, he did so in the expectation that he would be able to increase the club's crowds by attracting rugby league fans. To achieve this, Warren intended to transfer the club from Heywood Road, its home for 90 years, to the ground of a local rugby league club. The Willows, the home of Salford RLFC, was his first choice and Sale's management made contact. However, a combination of objections from Sale's members and a strong reluctance on the part of Salford's directors got in the way. Warren did not pursue his investment plans and as Sale's attendances stubbornly refused to increase to the point where a new ground was essential the chance to discover whether the rugby league fan base in south Lancashire would switch to union remained unproven.

Over on the eastern side of the Pennines that expectation was actually put to the test. Leeds RUFC's ground-breaking tenancy at Headingley began in September 1996 and even if it did not appear to prove that the Leeds crowd would take to the new game suddenly on offer, it did demonstrate the commercial possibilities of the arrangement. Most northern club owners, union and league, recognised that the Headingley arrangement had something to offer. For ambitious union clubs it provided a ground capable of accommodating far larger crowds should they materialise. For league it offered a partnership that could help fund the replacement or renovation of the many grounds that had fallen into disrepair. For a while it looked set to become a model that many northern clubs would adopt. Some fanciful schemes were floated, but by spring 1997 both Wakefield and Wigan had entered into serious negotiations with their leading union neighbours regarding closer working and possible sharing of new grounds. Down south, there was a similar hope that spectators might move, this time in the opposite direction when the London Broncos concluded an agreement for a three-year tenancy at The Stoop, the home of Harlequins RUFC, and are now poised to return there for the 2006 season. As the new Millennium approached, Bradford and St Helens were reportedly attempting to strike deals with union clubs to share their grounds. If those ground schemes had been made with an association football club there would have been little controversy; but because a union interest was involved they produced a feeling of unease in the league world.

Out of all these schemes there was only one where the two parties were brought together into an official partnership. It all started at the end of the first Super League summer season, when the cash strapped Leeds CF&AC, the owner of the Headingley complex and Leeds RLFC, was put up for sale and bought by local businessman and former Headingley RUFC first-teamer, Paul Caddick. During 1997, Caddick added his tenants, Leeds RUFC, to his rugby portfolio. Finally in July 1998, he moved beyond ground sharing and merged the two clubs, the Rhinos and what became the Tykes, into one company, Leeds Rugby Limited, which was described as the world's first rugby partnership. For the Tykes, the arrangement offered something more than just savings – it offered the chance to share players and to tap into a range of new skills. While player sharing never really proved a success when tried with the likes of the Australian rugby league international, Wendell Sailor, the savings were partially delivered in the form of an Academy where youth talent would be jointly nurtured.

There would have been another if Peter Deakin had had his way. Taking up his position as chief executive in February 1999, Deakin had as one of his major priorities to get the Warrington Wolves out of

Wilderspool and into a new stadium as soon as possible. He harboured hopes that a partnership could be developed that would see Sale transfer its professional operations to the town as the basis of a new merged super club. Opposition proved too strong at Warrington and Deakin joined Sale before trying again. This time Deakin tried to link the Sharks with the Salford City Reds. Despite Deakin's league background Salford, having already entered into negotiations with the local council to try and secure planning permission for a new stadium, had reservations about the approach. Interviewed in January 2001, David Tarry, Salford's chief executive, was concerned that if the council's approval was not forthcoming then the City Reds would be "at the mercy of other people who may not have our best interests at heart". Needless to say, that attempt was also doomed to failure. Shortly afterwards Deakin was enticed back to Saracens and the Sharks went on to follow other stadium sharing options. His untimely death denied him the chance to return for another go at building a combined club in the north-west.

In the brave new world of professional rugby union the leading clubs, like Sale, had had to restructure. New autonomous professional operations had been established, which had rapidly distanced themselves from their old amateur parent clubs. Those professional operations embraced a similar ethos to that which governed the thinking of Super League clubs. Namely that existing spectators must be kept happy, new ones won and that the best way to do that was to have the team serve up successful and open enterprising play. There seemed to be general agreement that what the spectators wanted was expansive handling moves that ended in tries, not long, drawn-out, set pieces. Being of a like mind the two rugby games found it easier to work together and union took the opportunity to learn and improve from league. The two games (in the north) appeared to fall into what could best be described as a seasonally adjusted relationship around which all kinds of sharing could go on. Union had the winter; league the summer. It was an arrangement that seemed to auger well for a harmonious future. Local partnerships began to spring up between leading league and union clubs to cover various aspects of their needs.

Nothing in rugby union's tradition was sacrosanct, certainly not when big money was involved. After protracted negotiation, Sale finally secured a major financial backer in May 2000. That backer was Brian Kennedy, a rugby union playing businessman, and his first major recruit, as chief executive, was Peter Deakin. Over the previous five years Deakin had built an impressive record of success in the marketing of professional rugby. Widely credited as the man who had masterminded the launch of the Bradford Bulls, Deakin subsequently turned around the ailing Saracens RUFC before returning to league with the Warrington Wolves. True to form, three months after he started work Deakin had his marketing plan

109

in place and the Sale Sharks were born, to take their place among all the other market driven rugby clubs.

Like many other clubs, Sale's most important early lesson from league was the understanding of what it meant to be a professional rugby club. Adrian Hadley, the former Welsh rugby union international, was recruited from Widnes RLFC as a player in spring 1996 and shortly afterwards promoted to team manager in a bid to bring some order into the squad. Later, Steve Hampson, a former league star with Wigan, Great Britain and latterly Salford RLFC's full-back, was brought in as a conditioner to improve the team's fitness. They worked together to imbue the club with new, professional standards of attitude, fitness and skills. One measure of progress was the rate at which new concepts like game plan, match statistics, defensive systems, weights programmes, diet schemes and video analysis were embedding themselves into the jargon of a union club like Sale. Another measure of progress was how quickly Sale's playing squad, which soon included a number of veteran former leaguers, began to take on a far more athletic appearance.

As the two games moved into the 21st century, it was clear to anyone going to a top level rugby match that in many ways union and league had begun to show signs of an uncanny resemblance. The club names, once so different, had begun to sound familiar. Some of the players, on occasion were identical. The competition very possibly had the same sponsor, the pre-match entertainment and the mascot were inevitably too familiar, the players running onto the field might have a similar athletic shape and the ground might well be the same, but once the ball was kicked off it was obvious that rugby still existed as two separate and different games. While the trappings of professionalism might have blurred the differences, the two games remained very competitive. Any idea that legalising professionalism alone would bring the games together was in practice little more than a pipe-dream.

There may have been plenty of examples of good local working relationships being fostered, but the overall relationship was never truly easy. The RFU's long term intentions remained a source of concern for many in rugby league. There was always a nagging doubt, no matter how many public expressions of respect for its players and supporters were forthcoming, that deep down the RFU would never accept that the RFL was here to stay. Relations looked to be better than ever when, after the closure of Wembley Stadium, the RFL was allowed to hire Twickenham for the opening match of its World Cup in October 2000 and then for the Centennial Challenge Cup Final six months later. In welcoming league to Twickenham, the RFU conveyed a very public impression of friendship while behind the scenes it appeared to be laying plans to decapitate its rival. In place of the previous disparate initiatives by individual club owners, there emerged a more deliberate, concerted campaign that was shaped by a few leading figures operating around Twickenham. Hiring

Twickenham ushered in a torrid 12 months that threatened for a time to set relations between the two games back 30 years.

For a majority within the leadership of the RFU, the slowly developing contacts between the two games were delivering too little too slowly. Rather than wait, they appear to have taken it upon themselves to flex their financial muscles and grab what they wanted from league. League's leading figures and clubs were targeted in the hope that in time the fans would follow. To prepare the ground for this raid, a concerted media campaign seemingly designed to try and acclimatise league's fans to the inevitable demise of their game moved into top gear. Every rumour, indeed every rumour of a rumour, linking a leading rugby league player to rugby union was seized upon and publicised. Rumours also circulated that the RFL and the RFU had held talks about a possible merger and these had to be denied by the RFL chairman, Rodney Walker in March 2001. Official talks did have to be arranged by Sport England the following month, but those were to try and restore working relations after accusations that the RFU was bypassing all conventions and directly contacting young league players.

Meanwhile, Clive Woodward, England rugby union's head coach, and his assistant, Phil Larder, the former British rugby league coach, were on the lookout for established players by a more orthodox route. An out of contract Jason Robinson proved receptive to Woodward's approaches and by mid-October 2000 Sale Sharks were able to announce that they had secured Robinson's services on England's behalf. Almost immediately, Robinson was fast-tracked into the England national squad and would go on to take a starring role for the British Lions the following summer.

England's coaching team had also recently been bolstered by the recruitment of Joe Lydon from the RFL's elite performance unit, initially as the England under-19 team manager. It would soon be further strengthened by the addition of Ellery Hanley as a defence coach. Jason Robinson's obviously successful switch to the union game convinced the Welsh RU to make funds available to its leading clubs to join the RFU in a further series of high profile raids on English league in the summer of 2001. For a while it appeared that open season had been declared on around a dozen of league's out of contract stars. Both Unions achieved initial success with Henry Paul's signature being confirmed by Gloucester RUFC in July 2001 and Iestyn Harris leaving the Rhinos for Cardiff the following month. Hopes of further recruits were dashed when two of the most high profile targets, Kris Radlinski and Keiron Cunningham, announced they had rejected huge offers from Sale Sharks and the RFU, and Swansea and the WRU respectively. Other, less well known players had already or would shortly make similar decisions.

While the bidding war raged, a number of Super League clubs were seriously planning to formalise links with rugby union clubs and Peter Wheeler took the opportunity in mid-July 2001 to spell out clearly how he hoped that this development would be fostered by the union's leadership. Wheeler, the chief executive of Leicester Tigers, took advantage of an interview with the *Sydney Morning Herald* to spell out what was going on back home. Apparently there had been a wide-ranging dialogue taking place for the past three years, but of late the points under discussion had concentrated on future relations. Negotiations had since been opened by the RFU and the Zurich Premiership clubs with a number of league clubs – the big four, Bradford Bulls, Leeds Rhinos, St Helens and Wigan Warriors were rumoured to be amongst them – the outcome of which Wheeler hoped would be the rapid expansion of rugby union operations in Lancashire and Yorkshire. He was very optimistic and hoped that one or two Super League clubs would decide to set up a union operation within a couple of months. These operations would be run in parallel with the parent league club and it was hoped to have all the interested clubs involved in a top-level union competition by September 2002. While none of the above was necessarily controversial, Wheeler's closing comments certainly were. Once those clubs' supporters could be won over to union in large numbers, Wheeler expected the partner league operation to be shut down!

When the news broke, it provoked immediate anger and Shane Richardson, the chief executive of Hull FC, demanded that those involved should declare themselves. Many non-involved clubs felt betrayed, knowing that a few of their number were secretly discussing possible switches to union, or some hybrid game, while contributing to the Super League's own review of the way forward. Arguably the RFU's campaign proved counter-productive, fuelling the suspicions of the majority of league fans' and increasing their commitment to the game rather than weakening it.

As the summer of 2001 turned to autumn, what had appeared to be a concerted assault on rugby league just petered out. Symbolically the announcement that a couple of very prominent players had rejected Union's advances marked the end of the recruitment drive. Its end also went some way to allay fears within league that it was effectively being demoted to the role of a feeder game for union – providing skilled players, talented coaches and new ideas on demand. Plans to introduce new senior union teams alongside Super League clubs in Yorkshire and Lancashire were quietly dropped. Relations were allowed to return to the professional normality they had enjoyed immediately after 1995, but without any guarantee they would stay that way.

It took a while for the mistrust to ebb away and contacts at top level became scarcer. Little was heard of any joint club activity at the Super League level. Things were different away from first team football and quite a number of rugby union clubs continued to provide regular homes

Rugby union: Zurich Premiership action – Newcastle versus Leeds Tykes.
(Photo: David Williams)

for Super League Academy teams. Occasional rumours and concerns surfaced in the media suggesting that a leading test player, generally Paul Sculthorpe, was being targeted by the RFU. Beyond the league test squad there may have been a few regrets expressed, but certainly no rancour if a player chose to accept union offers. Those extra career opportunities were eagerly seized by players like Phil Jones who, finding himself surplus to Wigan's requirements had spells with Orrell and Rotherham Titans before returning to Super League with Leigh Centurions.

Surprisingly what formal contact there was arose largely in response to a strong, perhaps sentimental, yearning for the two games to be brought together on the field of play. Of all the encounters of that first open union season, Wigan's victory in the Middlesex Sevens had provided a near perfect showcase for all of rugby league's best qualities. Unfortunately, Wigan did not return to defend their crown and the next couple of sides with league involvement to enter certainly did not grab the headlines. However, the value of participating was again demonstrated in August 2002 when the Bradford Bulls won England's premier tournament, drawing plaudits for their incisive running and sound defence. It was a worthy victory achieved in very difficult circumstances. Once the seasons got out of line union's start of season sevens tournaments fell into what is a critical time in the Super League programme and those members who have subsequently received invites have had to withdraw rather than risk jeopardising their main priorities.

Changes in season and difficulties matching players to the technical demands of the two games have largely ended XV-a-side contests. After the challenge matches between Bath and Wigan, no other reasonably high profile meeting took place for nearly seven years. When Sale and St Helens met in January 2003, the outcome was extremely predictable – each club won the half under their own rules. In the half under their opponents' rules each club played very negatively. To try and make it easier to achieve a result, that match was played using a standardised scoring system with tries counting for five points and all goals two. Addressing the scoring values was a small step forward, but no attempt was made to standardise any aspect of play.

It is obvious why the organisers of that match kept away from such a thorny area for all the old taboos about each game's respective laws were still in circulation. While those taboos continue to hold sway neither game has the freedom to openly state that its own laws might be improved if they incorporated aspects of its rival. What dialogue exists is highly emotional and partisan – with league being berated by its critics for its endless repetition while union stands accused of having mired itself in an ever deepening slough of technicalities. For there to be any point in continuing with XV-a-side challenge matches some hybrid form of playing rules, similar to those devised by Australian Rules and Gaelic Football to facilitate their meetings, would have to be developed. However, as both games value their independence and history so highly there is little chance of either of them agreeing to that kind of compromise.

Four years on, Peter Wheeler's observation that rugby union's expansion into the rugby league heartlands would be dependent on the attitude of the fans is truer than ever, although not perhaps in the way he had anticipated. Thanks to the recruitment of a high profile player like Jason Robinson and relocation to a better stadium at Stockport, Sale Sharks have consolidated their position in the top flight of English rugby union and have at last begun to attract the sort of attendances they need. Meanwhile Leeds Tykes, despite gaining promotion to the Zurich Premiership in 2001, have yet to achieve anything like equal standing with their stable mates the Rhinos. With the exception of those two, the experience since Wheeler gave that interview does not make good reading for union's administrators. Lack of support undermined the viability of what were once leading union clubs and eventually led Bradford Bulls and Wigan to sever contact with Wakefield RUFC and Orrell respectively. Starved of income, Wakefield subsequently collapsed and Orrell were handed back to a supporters' consortium. Even in a city the size of Leeds support for the Tykes has proved patchy and caused Paul Caddick to issue warnings regarding the club's long term viability.

114

With the exception of Headingley the two games at senior level remain divorced, although the London Broncos move to work closely with Harlequins in 2006 could replicate the Leeds example. Rather than let it be viewed as some form of eccentric oddity Headingley's pioneering partnership has had at least one official seal of approval conferred upon it. That recognition was forthcoming because, unlike anywhere else in the country, Leeds Rugby Limited is able to provide a real working point of contact for the two games.

When it came to getting the squad ready for the upcoming Six Nations Tournament the England rugby union coaching team chose to hold its training camp at Leeds in mid-January 2005. Hosted jointly by the Rhinos and the Tykes the three-day camp was designed to bring together different approaches and promote a crossover of skills. At the press conferences and on the training pitches there was plenty of evidence of mutual respect as the two sets of players and staff worked together. According to the Rhinos their expectations seemed to be limited to getting a greater insight into the finer arts of kicking from Dave Aldred, which, if that was the case might have helped get them closer to the tactical kicking abilities regularly displayed in the Australian National Rugby League. Their counterparts from the English rugby union squad were expecting far more from the sessions – to leave Leeds far sharper defensively and having regained the invention and vision that had been lost from their attacking play. Those benefits seem to have been thought achievable because there was talk when the sessions ended of running the camp annually.

While the vision of a rugby union game significantly enhanced through the incorporation of various league skills continues to be Twickenham's 'holy grail' it was always highly likely that further recruits, whether established or with great potential, would be sought. During his last Six Nations Tournament, Sir Clive Woodward found time in February 2004 to convince the Sale Sharks' management to accept the services of Joe Lydon, then the England Sevens coach, to help in the identification and development of local talent. Even after Woodward's departure, his successor, Andy Robinson, retained his former boss's vision and took it a step further as he sponsored the recruitment of Andy Farrell by Saracens in March 2005.

After his years of great service Farrell departed for his new challenge with a lot of league good will. He also received a ringing endorsement from Andy Robinson who paid him an amazing compliment, saying that Farrell could "... revolutionize rugby union in terms of the skills he brings". Whether Farrell can acclimatize to the union game quickly enough to meet these expectations is a huge unknown. However, the possibility that he might revolutionize his new game keeps open the possibility that at some point union may metamorphose into a game that league fans will want to watch. Could that development motivate the two games sufficiently to converge?

What is clear is that the willingness of English rugby's players, coaches, owners and executives to become far more open-minded has so far had no effect on either game's loyal fans, who remain quite hostile to the other game. In many ways those loyal fans are the custodians if not the true owners of their chosen game and it is they who will determine the future relationship of the two games. Over the course of the split they evolved into two distinct tribes, both equally partisan. While the level of passion shown by Leeds Rhinos' fans standing in Headingley's South Stand and the Leeds Tykes' fans who replace them on other match days might be very similar, there remains a wide gulf of mistrust between them. The personal investment made by generations of fans in their choice of club and game has not been undermined anywhere in the north of England. As a result, the fans' partisan outlook has remained almost totally unchanged over the first decade.

When league shifted to summer it had been hoped that with matches spread throughout the year league and union would no longer be competing directly and therefore fans could fill vacant match days watching the other game. This possibility could only become a reality if fans had respect for the other game, which was generally not the case, and very few League fans have been tempted to take advantage. Union does not have that respect because most league fans consider the play served up in the majority of its matches to be dull and boring. Union fans would undoubtedly counter by describing league as monotonous and predictable.

That entrenched partisanship was probably expected from rugby league fans, mainly for historical reasons. Their fierce local loyalty and pride has only too often been responsible for securing league's future in the face of some predator. Certainly the total disdain of Wigan's fans for Orrell's efforts severely limited the latter's ability to operate in the professional era. Similarly, whenever Headingley's management attempted to tempt Rhinos' fans into watching the Tykes, it has provoked, so far at best widespread disinterest and at worst hostile demonstrations. This was not an attitude restricted to the north of England. It could also be found in London where very few of the Harlequins' supporters appear to have taken the chance to watch the Broncos during their three year tenancy at the Stoop.

While the vast majority of fans cannot easily be tempted to switch from one form of rugby to another they are wary of change being introduced to their preferred game by the back door. Fans on both sides therefore, are, inherently suspicious of any proposed law change, fearing that it will sacrifice part of their heritage and take their chosen game in the direction of their rival. Consequently, bringing about convergence between the games on the field will be extremely difficult in the short and possibly even long term.

That will be good news to many league fans. They appreciate their game and the way it revolves around pace and movement. Union's set pieces and mauls are not for them. They do not want to see their game absorbed and lose its identity. They want the two games to keep their distance and retain as much as possible of the old status quo. If that can be maintained then as far as those fans are concerned the two games ought to be able to happily coexist side by side. The fans and their spending power whether on the terraces or watching at home are the key to the future of both games. At present they show little or no disposition towards questioning their allegiance.

Besides some occasional transfer of talent or skills, or a bit of ground sharing, what else has been achieved? Contrary to many initial expectations the two games have not moved towards reunification, perhaps because commercial interests were more intent on keeping them apart. After all, each game has developed separately for good reasons and to the staunchest sections of their support that is how they should remain. There is a lot to be said in support of that argument for each game has nurtured slightly different skills and focused on slightly different physical characteristics to create its own, quite different style of play. Despite the differences fans, as they have always done, continue to try and find evidence for which game is best. Players with playing experience of both are often pressed to give their verdict. As Iestyn Harris diplomatically replied when asked to compare the games when he returned to League at the start of July 2004, after three years with the Cardiff Blues; they are "both different and both great".

Critically, no one knows if the fans will ever be prepared to compromise. So far, sentiment has been unable to dislodge the central place that commerce and tradition hold in maintaining the current arrangements. Will there ever be another force strong enough to break that alliance? At this moment in time no one knows. So two games it is and it looks like two games it will stay.

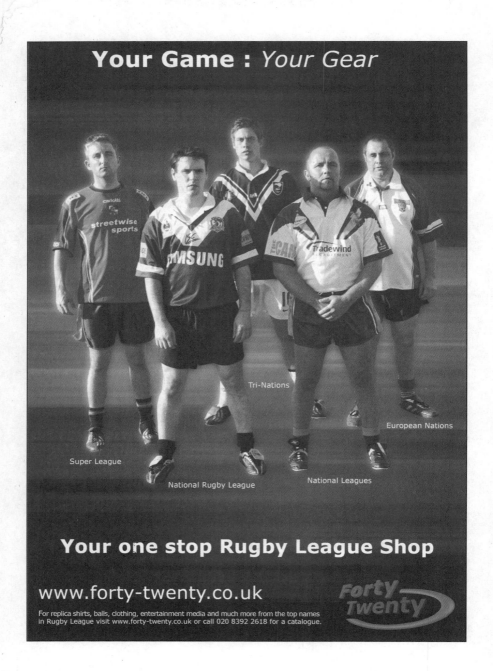